The BEST PLACES® *Northwest*
Desserts Cookbook

The BEST PLACES® *Northwest*

Desserts

Cookbook

SASQUATCH BOOKS
SEATTLE

Printed in Singapore by Star Standard Industries Pte Ltd.
Published by Sasquatch Books
Distributed by Publishers Group West
12 11 10 09 08 07 06 05 04   6 5 4 3 2 1

Book design: Kate Basart
Composition: Stewart A. Williams
Photography: Diane Padys

Library of Congress Cataloging-in-Publication Data

Nims, Cynthia C.
      The best places Northwest desserts cookbook : recipes from the best restaurants and inns of Washington, Oregon, and British Columbia / by Cynthia C. Nims.
            p.   cm.
      Includes index.
      ISBN 1-57061-410-5
    1.   Desserts. 2. Cookery, American--Pacific Northwest style. I. Title.
TX773.N56 2004
641.8'6--dc22   2004048150

Sasquatch Books / 119 South Main Street, Suite 400 / Seattle, WA 98104
(206) 467-4300 / www.sasquatchbooks.com / custserv@sasquatchbooks.com

Contents

Cakes

Double-Baked Chocolate Cake

THE WHITEHOUSE-CRAWFORD RESTAURANT, WALLA WALLA, WASHINGTON

This rich and luscious chocolate cake is great for entertaining because it can be prepared through the first baking, refrigerated, and then popped in the oven for the second baking just before serving. Chef Jamie Guerin, whose wife, pastry chef Sara Guerin, developed the recipe, uses Callebaut brand chocolate for this dessert, but any top-quality baking chocolate will produce excellent results. The dessert has an interesting blend of characteristics that are part cake, part brownie, part soufflé. If you're motivated to make your own ice cream to serve alongside, consider the Honey Rosemary Ice Cream (page 159) or Star Anise Ice Cream (page 153).

1 cup unsalted butter, cut into pieces

8 ounces top-quality bittersweet or semisweet chocolate, finely chopped

¾ cup unsweetened cocoa powder

7 eggs, separated

1⅓ cups sugar

Ice cream, for serving (optional)

Preheat the oven to 350°F. Butter a 9- to 10-inch springform pan and line the bottom with a round of parchment paper. Butter the paper, dust the pan with flour, and tap out excess.

Melt the butter in a medium saucepan over medium-low heat. Take the pan from the heat, add the chocolate, and whisk gently until fully melted. Add the cocoa powder and whisk until smooth.

Whip the egg yolks with ⅔ cup of the sugar in an electric mixer at medium-high speed until pale and light, about 3 minutes. Put the egg-yolk mixture into a large bowl and wash and dry the mixer's bowl and beaters well. Whip

the egg whites at medium-high speed until soft peaks form. Gradually add the remaining ⅔ cup sugar and whip until the whites are stiff and glossy.

Using a rubber spatula, fold the chocolate into the egg-yolk mixture until barely combined. Fold in the egg whites just until no white streaks remain. Spoon 2 cups of the batter into a medium bowl and refrigerate. Scrape the remaining batter into the prepared pan and smooth the top. Bake until the cake is puffed and a toothpick inserted in the center comes out clean, 35 to 40 minutes. Let cool completely on a wire rack.

When the cake is cool, remove the sides of the springform pan and spread the reserved cake batter over the top of the cake, leaving a 1-inch border around the edge. Refrigerate the cake for at least 1 hour.

Shortly before serving, preheat the oven to 425°F.

Bake the cake until a thin crust forms on top and the batter is soft and creamy beneath the crust, 10 to 12 minutes. Let the cake cool on a wire rack for about 15 minutes. Cut into wedges and serve warm, with ice cream if you like.

Makes 12 to 16 servings

Lemon Olive Oil Cake

BACCHUS RISTORANTE, VANCOUVER, BRITISH COLUMBIA

This moist, aromatic cake is an easy and not-too-sweet option for dessert or a great accompaniment for an afternoon cup of tea. Delicious as is, it would be extra tasty topped with fresh berries and a dollop of whipped cream or drizzled with a simple glaze of lemon juice with powdered sugar. Pure olive oil, rather than the more deeply flavored extra virgin olive oil, is the better choice for this cake.

1¾ cups all-purpose flour

1 tablespoon baking powder

½ teaspoon salt

1½ cups sugar

4 teaspoons finely grated lemon zest

2 teaspoons finely grated orange zest

4 eggs

¼ cup freshly squeezed lemon juice

3 tablespoons whipping cream

¾ cup pure olive oil

Preheat the oven to 300° F. Butter and flour a 9-inch square or round cake pan.

Sift together the flour, baking powder, and salt, and set aside. Combine the sugar, lemon zest, and orange zest in a medium bowl and rub the mixture between your hands until fragrant and moist. Cream together the sugar mixture and eggs in an electric mixer fitted with the paddle attachment. Slowly add the lemon juice and cream and mix until blended. Add the dry

ingredients in 3 parts, alternating with the olive oil in 2 parts, and mix until blended. Pour the batter into the prepared pan and bake until a toothpick inserted in the center comes out clean, 50 to 60 minutes.

MAKES 8 TO 10 SERVINGS

Rhubarb-Cornmeal Upside-Down Cake

HIGGINS RESTAURANT AND BAR, PORTLAND, OREGON

Cornmeal adds a delightful slightly nutty texture and flavor to this cake, a great complement to the slightly caramelized rhubarb topping. For an easy home-style baking method, the cake can be made in a cast-iron skillet. Melt the butter directly in the skillet, add the brown sugar, and continue as directed for the cake pan.

1¼ cups all-purpose flour

1 cup fine cornmeal

4 teaspoons baking powder

½ teaspoon salt

½ cup unsalted butter, at room temperature

1¼ cups granulated sugar

2 eggs

2 teaspoons vanilla extract

Grated zest of 1 lemon

¾ cup plus 2 tablespoons milk

Lightly sweetened whipped cream, for serving

Rhubarb Topping

½ cup unsalted butter

¾ cup packed light brown sugar

4 large stalks rhubarb (about 1 pound), trimmed and cut into 2-inch sticks

Preheat the oven to 350°F. Butter a 10-inch cake pan.

For the rhubarb topping, melt the butter in a medium skillet over medium heat, stir in the brown sugar, and spread the glaze mixture evenly on the bottom of the cake pan. Arrange the rhubarb pieces snugly in a single layer in the cake pan and bake to soften them slightly, about 10 minutes. Set aside on a wire rack and leave the oven set at 350°F.

Combine the flour, cornmeal, baking powder, and salt in a medium bowl and stir well to evenly mix. Cream together the room-temperature butter and sugar with an electric mixer at medium speed. Add one of the eggs and beat well, scraping down the sides of the bowl before beating in the second egg. Beat in the vanilla and lemon zest. Slowly mix in the dry ingredients in a few batches, alternating with the milk. Spoon the batter over the rhubarb and spread it evenly. Bake until the top is lightly browned and a toothpick inserted in the center comes out clean, 25 to 30 minutes.

Let the cake cool on a wire rack for about 15 minutes. Set a serving plate upside down on the cake pan and quickly but carefully invert them both together, gently lifting off the cake pan so that the cooking liquids drip down onto the cake. Serve warm with whipped cream.

MAKES 8 TO 12 SERVINGS

Chocolate Hazelnut Torte

GEISER GRAND HOTEL, BAKER CITY, OREGON

The hazelnuts used at the Geiser Grand Hotel for this torte come from Yamhill County in western Oregon, where virtually all of the country's hazelnuts are grown. It will be easiest to handle the assembly and service of the cake if you assemble it on a round of cardboard for easy moving. Specialty shops carry heavy-duty cardboard rounds used by pastry chefs, though you can cut a round just slightly smaller than the diameter of the cake and cover it with foil before using.

1½ cups toasted skinned hazelnuts (see page 68)

1 cup sugar

½ cup all-purpose flour

½ teaspoon salt

¾ cup unsalted butter, at room temperature

6 ounces top-quality bittersweet chocolate, chopped

6 ounces top-quality semisweet chocolate, chopped

2 ounces top-quality white chocolate, chopped

8 eggs, separated

2 teaspoons vanilla extract

½ teaspoon cream of tartar

Chocolate curls, for garnish (see page 12)

Toasted skinned whole hazelnuts, for garnish

Hazelnut Filling

¼ cup sugar

2 tablespoons water

2 tablespoons Frangelico

½ cup unsalted butter

½ cup whipping cream

1¼ cups toasted skinned hazelnuts, finely chopped

2 tablespoons honey

Ganache Topping

1¼ cups whipping cream

4 ounces top-quality bittersweet chocolate, chopped

4 ounces top-quality semisweet chocolate, chopped

2 ounces top-quality white chocolate, chopped

For the hazelnut filling, combine the sugar, water, and Frangelico in a small heavy saucepan and cook over medium-high heat until the mixture turns a light amber color, about 5 minutes. Add the butter and cream and simmer, stirring occasionally, for 15 minutes. Remove the pan from the heat and stir in the hazelnuts and honey. Let cool completely at room temperature.

Preheat the oven to 375°F. Butter two 9-inch cake pans and line the bottom of each with a round of parchment paper (see page 156).

For the cake, combine the hazelnuts and ¼ cup of the sugar in a food processor and pulse to finely chop. Transfer the nuts to a medium bowl, stir in the flour and salt, and set aside. Melt the butter and 3 chocolates in the top of a double boiler or in a heatproof bowl set over a pan of simmering (not boiling) water, stirring occasionally until smooth. In a large bowl, whisk the egg yolks with the remaining ¾ cup of the sugar. Whisk in the melted chocolate mixture and vanilla. Fold in the hazelnut-flour mixture.

Beat the egg whites and cream of tartar with an electric mixer at high speed until stiff but not dry. Fold a big spoonful of the egg whites into the chocolate batter to lighten it, then gently fold in the remaining whites. Divide the batter between the prepared pans and bake until a toothpick inserted in the center comes out clean, 30 to 35 minutes. Let the cakes cool on a wire rack.

For the ganache, heat the cream in a small saucepan over medium-high heat until bubbles form around the edges. Put the chopped chocolates in a medium bowl and add the hot cream. Let sit for 5 minutes and stir until smooth. Let cool to room temperature.

Unmold the cakes, discard the paper, and trim the tops if needed so that they are flat. Put one of the cakes on a cardboard round, if using, then on a wire rack set over a rimmed baking sheet. Spread the filling on the cake and set the second cake on top, pressing down gently. Pour the chocolate ganache topping over the cake, slowly covering the top so that it drizzles evenly down the sides as well. (The ganache should be pourable. If it isn't, rewarm it slightly.) Use a rubber spatula to guide the ganache into any openings on the sides of the cake. Decorate with chocolate curls and whole hazelnuts. Chill on a wire rack in the refrigerator until firm, about 4 hours. Run a knife under the cake to loosen it from the rack and set it on a serving platter to serve.

Makes 16 to 20 servings

Chocolate Curls

To make chocolate curls as garnish for this and any number of chocolate desserts, simply draw a vegetable peeler along the long side of a piece of top-quality semisweet chocolate. (The thicker the piece of chocolate, the broader your curls will be.) Work over a piece of waxed paper or foil to catch the curls. Lift that up to scatter the curls rather than doing so with your hands, which might melt the chocolate.

Black Bear Ginger Cake

MANNING PARK RESORT, HOPE, BRITISH COLUMBIA

L ast winter I was trying to think of a dessert that would be tasty and give you that warm, comfortable feeling of home when you got a whiff of it," explains executive chef Christian Collins. He found his late mom's recipe for warm ginger cake and made some modifications, including the addition of the candied ginger for extra ginger flavor. The results are indeed comfort food at its best.

The nearby Bear Brewing in Kamloops brews a Black Bear Ale subtly flavored with blackberries and black currants, which the chef uses in place of the dark beer that the original recipe called for, though other dark ales can be used instead. "We like to keep this a special treat, so we only make it seasonally, from December to April," notes Collins. He bakes the dessert in individual one-cup dishes, but this larger one-dish variation is a snap to assemble, great for a crowd. The cake's caramel sauce makes for a grand finish.

1 cup Black Bear Ale or other dark beer or stout

1 cup molasses

1½ teaspoons baking soda

3 eggs

½ cup granulated sugar

½ cup packed dark brown sugar

¾ cup vegetable oil

2 cups all-purpose flour

2 tablespoons powdered ginger

1½ teaspoons baking powder

¾ teaspoon ground cinnamon

¼ teaspoon ground cloves

¼ teaspoon freshly grated or ground nutmeg

⅛ teaspoon ground cardamom

12 pieces candied ginger, roughly dime-sized

Caramel Sauce

¾ cup whipping cream

¼ cup unsalted butter, cut into small pieces

1½ cups granulated sugar

¼ cup plus 2 tablespoons water

Preheat the oven to 375°F. Lightly butter a 9- by 13-inch baking dish.

Combine the beer and molasses in a medium saucepan over high heat and bring to a boil, stirring occasionally. Take the pan from the heat and sprinkle the baking soda over but do not stir; foam will rise in the pan. Set aside to cool for about 15 minutes.

Whisk together the eggs, granulated sugar, and brown sugar in a medium bowl until well blended. Whisk in the oil. Stir together the flour, powdered ginger, baking powder, cinnamon, cloves, nutmeg, and cardamom in a large bowl.

Whisk the beer mixture into the egg mixture, then whisk this into the dry ingredients in 2 batches. Pour the batter into the baking dish and scatter the candied ginger evenly over the top. Bake until the top springs back when gently pressed, 25 to 30 minutes. Transfer to a wire rack to cool.

For the caramel sauce, combine the cream and butter in a small saucepan and warm over medium-low heat until the butter melts. Keep warm over low heat. Combine the sugar and water in a medium saucepan and cook over medium-high heat, gently swirling the pan occasionally; do not stir. Use

a pastry brush dipped in water to brush down any sugar crystals that form on the sides of the pan. Let the mixture boil until it becomes deep golden brown. Take the pan from the heat and slowly whisk in the warm cream-butter mixture. Be careful of the very hot steam that rises. Set the caramel aside to cool. Either use right away or store in an airtight container, refrigerated, until ready to serve.

To serve, cut the cake into squares and set them on individual plates, drizzle caramel sauce over and around, and serve.

Makes 12 servings

Lemon Pudding Cakes with Blackberry–Pinot Noir Coulis

BARKING FROG, WOODINVILLE, WASHINGTON

There's an intriguing split-level finish to this dessert, a creamy pudding topping and an ethereal light cake—a magic metamorphosis that comes from one easy-to-make batter. If fresh blackberries are not available, frozen may be used, but the sugar quantity may need to be adjusted and a little water added at the start of cooking to keep the sugar from burning.

Superfine sugar is a standard ingredient in pastry kitchens, available with other baking goods in well-stocked grocery stores. The very fine-grain sugar melts much more quickly than regular granulated sugar. (Hint: It's also a great option for iced tea, cocktails, and anytime you're sweetening cold ingredients.)

¾ cup plus 2 teaspoons superfine sugar

3 tablespoons all-purpose flour

¼ teaspoon plus a pinch salt

1 cup buttermilk

3 eggs, separated

¼ cup freshly squeezed lemon juice

Candied Lemon Zest

1 large or 2 small lemons

1 cup granulated sugar

1 cup water

Blackberry–Pinot Noir Coulis

2 pints fresh blackberries, plus more for garnish

¾ cup granulated sugar

½ cup pinot noir

¼ teaspoon ground allspice

Pinch freshly grated or ground nutmeg

For the candied lemon zest, zest the lemon(s) using a zester—not a grater—or by peeling them with a vegetable peeler, peeling mostly just the outer vivid yellow layer and avoiding the white pith underneath. Cut the zest into fine julienne strips. Bring a small pan of water to a boil, add the zest, and blanch for 30 seconds. Drain the zest and repeat this 2 more times with fresh water, which helps draw away bitterness from the zest. Combine the sugar and 1 cup water in a small saucepan and bring to a boil over medium-high heat, stirring occasionally to help the sugar dissolve. Add the blanched zest and simmer until the zest is translucent, 5 to 8 minutes. Take the pan from the heat and let the zest cool to room temperature in the syrup; set aside. (The zest can be kept in the syrup in the refrigerator for up to 3 days.)

For the coulis, combine the blackberries, ½ cup of the sugar, ¼ cup of the pinot noir, the allspice, and nutmeg in a large saucepan over medium heat. Cook, stirring occasionally, until the berries start softening and releasing juice, about 15 minutes. Purée the mixture in a blender or food processor and strain through a fine sieve to remove the seeds. Return the berry mixture to the saucepan and add the remaining ¼ cup sugar and ¼ cup pinot noir. Cook for just long enough to dissolve the sugar and blend the flavors. Pour the coulis into a bowl and let cool. Refrigerate until ready to use.

Preheat the oven to 375°F. Very lightly oil eight ½-cup ramekins. Dust them with sugar and tap out excess. Set aside.

In a large bowl, whisk together the sugar, flour, and ¼ teaspoon of the salt. In a separate bowl, whisk together the buttermilk, egg yolks, and lemon juice. Whip the egg whites with the remaining pinch of the salt in an electric mixer at medium-high speed to stiff peaks. Stir the yolk mixture into the dry ingredients, and then, using a whisk, gently fold the egg whites into the batter. Pour the batter into the ramekins. (The batter has a tendency to separate, so you may need to rewhisk it to bring it together again as you go.) Put the filled ramekins in a roasting pan or baking dish, put it in the oven, and add enough boiling water to the pan to come halfway up the sides of the ramekins. Bake until the cakes are puffed (they will rise up above the rims like a soufflé), lightly golden, and the tops are dry to the touch, 16 to 20 minutes.

Let the cakes cool on a wire rack, still in the water bath, for at least 30 minutes. Take the ramekins from the water bath and chill them in the refrigerator for at least 2 hours before serving.

To serve, set a dessert plate upside-down on top of a ramekin. Holding both securely together, quickly flip them over and lift off the ramekin. If you need to, you can jiggle the ramekin to loosen the cake. Repeat with remaining ramekins. Drizzle the coulis around the cakes and sprinkle the coulis with a few blackberries. Lift the candied lemon zest from the syrup with a fork and set it on top of the cakes. Serve right away.

Makes 8 servings

Orange Cranberry Torte

HARRISON HOUSE BED AND BREAKFAST, CORVALLIS, OREGON

T his cake was a favorite from my childhood when my mother made it at holiday time," notes owner Maria Tomlinson, who finds it also a wonderful addition to breakfast offerings. The cake will keep well, up to two weeks, when well wrapped and refrigerated, making it convenient for casual dinners and drop-in guests. The glaze-like syrup soaks into the cake overnight, making a slightly denser, richer texture, though it is also delicious served right away if you're not too patient!

2¼ cups all-purpose flour

2 cups sugar

1 teaspoon baking powder

1 teaspoon baking soda

¼ teaspoon salt

1½ cups whole fresh cranberries (about ½ bag)

1 cup chopped walnuts or pecans

Grated zest of 2 oranges (about 2 tablespoons)

2 eggs

1 cup buttermilk

¾ cup vegetable oil

1 cup freshly squeezed orange juice

Lightly sweetened whipped cream, for serving (optional)

Preheat the oven to 350°F. Generously butter a 10-inch tube or Bundt pan.

Stir together the flour, 1 cup of the sugar, the baking powder, baking soda, and salt in a medium bowl. Stir in the cranberries, nuts, and orange zest. In

a separate medium bowl, lightly whisk the eggs to blend, then whisk in the buttermilk and oil until smooth. Add the wet ingredients to the dry ingredients and stir until evenly blended. Pour the batter into the prepared pan and bake until deep golden brown and a toothpick inserted in the center comes out clean, 45 to 55 minutes.

While the cake is baking, combine the remaining 1 cup of sugar and orange juice in a small saucepan and warm over medium heat, stirring just until the sugar is dissolved, 2 to 3 minutes. Set aside.

When the cake is done, take it from the oven and let it partly cool on a wire rack, about 15 minutes. Set the wire rack over a rimmed baking sheet and unmold the cake, upside down, onto the rack. Pour about half of the orange glaze slowly and evenly over the cake. Flip the cake over so that the top is facing up and pour the remaining glaze over the cake. Let cool completely. Wrap the cake in foil and refrigerate for 24 hours before cutting into slices to serve. Serve slices by themselves or with whipped cream if you like.

Makes 12 to 16 servings

Mojito Cheesecake

A longtime favorite, the cheesecake, is dressed up with the flavors of a more recent favorite—the mojito, a rum-mint-lime cocktail that originated on the sunny shores of Cuba. It's important to let the cream cheese soften at room temperature before blending, so that the cheesecake batter will be as creamy-smooth as possible.

1½ pounds cream cheese, at room temperature

1 cup granulated sugar

½ cup sour cream

4 eggs

⅓ cup dark rum

¼ cup limeade concentrate

Crust

2 cups fine graham cracker crumbs

6 tablespoons packed light brown sugar

½ cup unsalted butter, melted

Topping

1½ cups sour cream

6 tablespoons granulated sugar

2½ tablespoons finely chopped mint

Preheat the oven to 325°F.

For the crust, combine the graham cracker crumbs and brown sugar in a medium bowl and stir to mix. Add the melted butter and stir well. Press the mixture evenly into the bottom and about 1 inch up the sides of a 9- or 10-inch springform pan; set aside.

Blend the cream cheese in the bowl of an electric mixer fitted with the paddle attachment until smooth. Add the sugar and sour cream and continue beating until evenly blended. Add the eggs, one at a time, mixing well after each addition and scraping the sides of the bowl as needed. Add the rum and limeade concentrate and blend gently to evenly mix, scrape the bowl one last time, and mix again to make sure the batter is smooth. Pour the batter onto the crust and bake until the filling is set (when it no longer jiggles in the center when the pan is gently shaken), about 40 minutes. Turn the oven off and leave the cake in the closed oven for 1 hour.

Take the cheesecake from the oven and let cool to room temperature. Refrigerate until fully chilled, at least 3 hours or, preferably, overnight.

For the topping, preheat the oven to 350°F. Combine the sour cream and sugar in a small bowl and stir until smooth. Stir in the mint. Pour the topping over the cooled cheesecake, spread it out evenly, and bake until nearly set, 10 to 12 minutes. Refrigerate the cheesecake again to allow the topping to fully set. Remove the sides of the pan and cut into wedges to serve.

MAKES 16 TO 20 SERVINGS

Chocolate Raspberry Cake

West, Vancouver, British Columbia

From pastry chef Rhonda Viani comes this wonderfully moist chocolate cake celebrating that oh-so-delicious flavor combo of chocolate and raspberries. For the purée, start with about 8 ounces of fresh berries and purée them in a food processor or blender. Press the purée through a fine sieve to remove the many seeds; this should give you just about the ½ cup of strained purée needed for the cake. A scoop of vanilla bean ice cream would be great alongside, or try Viani's Raspberry Swirl Ice Cream (page 168) made with this cake in mind.

2 ounces top-quality bittersweet chocolate, chopped

1¼ cups sugar

⅓ cup vegetable oil

2 eggs

½ cup raspberry purée

½ cup all-purpose flour

⅓ cup unsweetened cocoa powder

½ teaspoon baking soda

¼ teaspoon salt

¼ cup sour cream

Fresh raspberries, for serving

Preheat the oven to 350°F. Lightly grease a 9-inch square or round baking pan and line the bottom with parchment paper.

Melt the chocolate in the top of a double boiler or in a heatproof bowl set over a pan of simmering (not boiling) water, stirring until smooth. Take the chocolate from the heat and set aside to cool slightly.

Whisk together the sugar and oil in a large bowl. Whisk in the eggs, one at a time, then whisk in the raspberry purée until evenly blended. In a separate bowl, sift together the flour, cocoa powder, baking soda, and salt.

Add the warm melted chocolate to the wet ingredients and whisk to combine. Add the dry ingredients in 3 parts with the sour cream in 2 parts, mixing well to ensure there are no lumps. Pour the batter into the prepared pan and bake until a toothpick inserted in the center comes out clean, about 35 minutes. Let cool to room temperature on a wire rack. Refrigerate until fully chilled before serving.

To serve, unmold the cake onto a cutting board and remove the parchment paper. Cut the cake into squares or wedges and arrange on individual plates, with a scattering of fresh raspberries around.

MAKES 8 SERVINGS

Cranberry Upside-Down Cake

HUDSON'S BAR AND GRILL, VANCOUVER, WASHINGTON

This is a delectable, simple use for the ruby red cranberries that grow in southwestern Washington State. The dessert, created by pastry chef Cheryl Rogers, was served at the famous James Beard House in New York. She accompanied executive chef Mark Hosack for his "guest chef" visit to the famed Oregon gastronome's former Big Apple home. At Hudson's, the cake is served with a simple crème anglaise sauce poured around just before serving.

½ cup whipping cream

2 eggs

¾ cup granulated sugar

Finely grated zest of 1 orange (about 1 tablespoon)

½ teaspoon vanilla extract

1 cup all-purpose flour

1 teaspoon baking powder

¼ teaspoon salt

Topping

⅓ cup granulated sugar

⅓ cup packed light brown sugar

6 tablespoons unsalted butter

1½ cups whole fresh cranberries (about ½ bag)

Preheat the oven to 350°F. Generously butter a 9-inch cake pan.

For the topping, combine the granulated sugar, brown sugar, and butter in a small saucepan and cook over medium heat until the sugars dissolve, about 5 minutes, stirring constantly. Pour the mixture into the cake pan and sprinkle the cranberries evenly over. Set aside.

Beat the cream in an electric mixer at medium-high speed until stiff. Add the eggs, sugar, orange zest, and vanilla and beat until well blended. In a small bowl, stir together the flour, baking powder, and salt. Fold the dry ingredients into the wet ingredients to blend evenly, then pour the batter over the cranberries. Bake until the cake is lightly browned on top and a toothpick inserted in the center comes out clean, about 30 minutes. Let the cake sit on a wire rack for 5 minutes. Put a serving plate upside down on the cake pan and quickly flip them both together. Slowly lift off the cake pan, allowing the caramelized cranberry mixture to drizzle down onto the cake. Cut into wedges to serve warm.

MAKES 8 SERVINGS

Almond Tea Cake

This no-fuss recipe is a great option for a quick after-school snack or an afternoon tea party with steaming pots of Earl Grey. The cake would also make a good, easy addition to a weekend brunch buffet. Any leftover cake will keep for up to a week, wrapped well in plastic.

⅔ cup packed light brown sugar

⅔ cup granulated sugar

⅔ cup vegetable oil

½ teaspoon salt

2 eggs

1 cup buttermilk

1¼ cups all-purpose flour

½ teaspoon baking soda

½ teaspoon baking powder

½ teaspoon almond extract

½ cup sliced almonds

Glaze

½ cup powdered sugar

2 tablespoons water

½ teaspoon vanilla extract

Preheat the oven to 350°F. Butter a 9- by 13-inch baking dish.

Stir together the brown sugar, granulated sugar, oil, and salt in a large bowl. Add the eggs and ½ cup of the buttermilk and stir until smooth and evenly blended. In a separate bowl, stir together the flour, baking soda, and baking powder, then stir the dry ingredients into the wet ingredients, followed by the remaining ½ cup buttermilk and the almond extract. Pour the batter into the baking pan (it will only be about 1 inch deep). Sprinkle the sliced almonds evenly over and bake until golden brown and a toothpick inserted in the center comes out clean, 20 to 22 minutes. Let cool slightly on a wire rack.

For the glaze, stir together the powdered sugar, water, and vanilla until smooth. Drizzle the glaze over the cake while still warm. Let the glaze set before cutting the cake into squares to serve.

MAKES 16 TO 20 SERVINGS

Banana Cake

Monsoon, Seattle, Washington

*T*his cake has quite a different texture than you might expect, a very moist, nearly jellylike quality that is found in many Asian desserts. It is best freshly made, while still a little warm from the oven.

1 cup sugar

4 tablespoons unsalted butter, at room temperature

3 overripe bananas, mashed

2 eggs

¼ cup freshly squeezed orange juice

½ cup all-purpose flour

1 teaspoon baking soda

Pinch salt

Coconut Sauce

1 cup coconut milk

1 tablespoon sugar

Pinch salt

1 teaspoon cornstarch dissolved in 1 tablespoon water

Preheat the oven to 350°F. Butter an 8- or 9-inch square baking pan.

Cream together the sugar and butter in the bowl of an electric mixer at medium speed. Add the mashed bananas, eggs, and orange juice and mix until evenly blended. In a separate bowl, stir together the flour, baking soda,

and salt. Slowly add the dry ingredients to the banana batter, mixing as you go, and scraping down the sides of the bowl. Pour the batter into the prepared pan and bake until set and lightly crispy around the edges, about 50 to 60 minutes.

For the sauce, heat the coconut milk in a small saucepan over medium heat. Add the sugar and salt and stir to dissolve. Add the dissolved cornstarch and stir until the sauce is thick enough to coat the back of a spoon, about 5 minutes. Pour the sauce into individual bowls.

To serve, cut the cake in half, then cut across into slices about ¾ inch thick. Arrange the warm slices on individual plates, with the small bowls of warm coconut sauce alongside for dipping the cake.

Makes 6 servings

Dreamsicle

EARTH AND OCEAN, SEATTLE, WASHINGTON

Dreamy, indeed, the kind of drink that you'll want to have right before crawling into bed for a night of sweet dreams. An optional addition is a little scoop of vanilla ice cream just before serving, a contrast of cold and hot that results in an even creamier drink.

8 ounces boiling water

1 Earl Grey tea bag

3 ounces Vermeer Dutch Chocolate liqueur

Vanilla ice cream (optional)

Pour the boiling water over the tea bag in a large coffee cup and let sit until steeped to your taste. Remove the tea bag, squeezing to remove excess water. Add the liqueur to the cup. Top with a scoop of ice cream, if desired, and serve.

MAKES 1 SERVING

Chocolate Decadence
with Strawberry Sauce

MOUNTAIN HOME LODGE, LEAVENWORTH, WASHINGTON

Executive chef Tom Obregon notes that this recipe is a favorite with guests at the lodge. The rich, dense, nearly flourless chocolate cake is a true indulgence, served with a bright, fresh strawberry sauce and a dollop of light whipped cream. The chef suggests freezing the baked cake for a day (or up to a few weeks) before serving, which helps the delicate cake firm up before cutting.

1 pound top-quality bittersweet chocolate, chopped

1½ cups unsalted butter, cut into small pieces

6 eggs

¼ cup plus 1 tablespoon granulated sugar, or more to taste

1 tablespoon all-purpose flour

1 cup whipping cream

¾ cup powdered sugar

½ teaspoon vanilla extract

8 ounces fresh strawberries, hulled

1 tablespoon brandy

Preheat the oven to 350°F. Line a 9-inch cake pan with a round of parchment paper.

Melt the chocolate and butter in the top of a double boiler or in a heatproof bowl set over a pan of simmering (not boiling) water, stirring until smooth. When melted, take the pan from the heat and set aside, still over the water to keep warm.

Whisk together the eggs and 1 tablespoon of the sugar in another double boiler or in another bowl set over a pan of simmering water, whisking constantly until the mixture is warm to the touch (about 130°F), about 5 minutes. Transfer this mixture right away to the bowl of a mixer and whip at medium speed until it cools a bit and is fluffy and thick.

Fold the melted chocolate mixture into the egg mixture until evenly blended. Sift the flour evenly over the batter and gently fold it in. Pour the batter into the prepared cake pan and bake until firm around the edges and the surface looks dry, about 10 minutes. Let cool on a wire rack. Wrap the cake (still in its pan) in plastic and freeze overnight.

Shortly before serving, take the cake from the freezer and unwrap it. Whip the cream with the powdered sugar and vanilla until stiff peaks form. Combine the strawberries with the remaining ¼ cup of the granulated sugar and the brandy in a blender or food processor and process until smooth. Taste for sweetness, adding a bit more sugar if needed to suit your taste. Strain the sauce to remove the seeds.

To serve, dip the base of the cake pan in a shallow dish of hot water, then turn the cake out into a serving platter, discarding the parchment. Frost the top of the cake with the whipped cream, leaving the sides unfrosted. Cut the cake into wedges and arrange on individual plates, spooning the strawberry sauce around.

MAKES 16 SERVINGS

Bayou Cheesecake

FROM THE BAYOU, PARKLAND, WASHINGTON

N ot that most cheesecakes aren't rich to begin with, but this variation manages to up the ante a bit with such additions as coconut, chocolate chips, and almonds. It is quite a treat, but pace yourself! This is the most popular dessert on From the Bayou's menu, baked daily to assure their guests a generous supply.

1½ pounds cream cheese, at room temperature

1 cup sugar

3 eggs

1 package (14 ounces) sweetened shredded coconut

1 package (12 ounces) milk chocolate chips

½ cup plus 2 tablespoons slivered almonds, toasted

1 teaspoon vanilla extract

1½ ounces top-quality semisweet chocolate, chopped

Crust

1½ cups fine chocolate wafer crumbs (about 30 cookies)

3 tablespoons sugar

¼ cup unsalted butter, melted

Preheat the oven to 350°F.

For the crust, stir together the cookie crumbs and sugar in a medium bowl. Add the melted butter and toss to mix. Press the crumbs into the bottom of a 9- or 10-inch springform pan and bake for 8 minutes. Set aside on a wire rack to cool. Leave the oven set at 350°F.

Cream together the cream cheese and sugar in an electric mixer at medium speed until light and fluffy. Add the eggs one at a time, beating well after each addition and scraping down the sides of the bowl as needed. Use a rubber spatula to stir in the coconut, chocolate chips, ½ cup of the almonds, and the vanilla. Pour the mixture onto the prepared crust and bake until the edges of the cheesecake are set and lightly browned, about 1 hour. Let cool on a wire rack.

When the cheesecake has cooled, melt the semisweet chocolate in a small heatproof bowl set over a pan of simmering (not boiling) water, stirring occasionally until smooth. Drizzle the melted chocolate in random swirls over the top of the cake. Sprinkle with the remaining 2 tablespoons slivered almonds. Refrigerate the cake until fully chilled, at least 8 hours. Remove the sides of the pan and cut the cheesecake into wedges to serve.

MAKES 16 TO 20 SERVINGS

Custards, Mousses & Puddings

Wild Huckleberry Crème Brûlée —38

Triple Layer Chocolate Martini—40

◄ *Chocolate and Brandied Dried-Cherry Bread Pudding*—42

Coconut Crème Caramel —46

Basil Panna Cotta with Strawberries—48

Maple, Orange, and Ginger Rice Custard—50

Tiramisu—54

Bread Pudding with Plum-Port Sauce—56

Wild Huckleberry Crème Brûlée

THE SHOALWATER RESTAURANT, SEAVIEW, WASHINGTON

The Long Beach Peninsula plays host to wild berries of all kinds. One of the favorites of chef-owner Ann Kischner is the tiny blue huckleberry that ripens in late summer. "They are prolific bearers, which is fortunate considering how quickly these crème brûlées sell!" she says. The berries freeze well for use in the winter, so stock up when they're available. You could use blueberries or other small berries, if you're unable to find huckleberries.

While standard ramekins can be used for this dessert, shallower and broader ceramic dishes are preferable so the caramelized topping has a maximum of surface area. A blowtorch, now thankfully available in a small, kitchen-friendly size, is the ideal tool for forming the perfect crisp topping.

1 cup wild blue huckleberries, plus more for garnish

7 egg yolks

⅓ cup sugar, plus more for caramelizing

Pinch salt

2½ cups whipping cream

½ teaspoon vanilla extract

Unsweetened whipped cream, for serving

Mint sprigs, for garnish

Preheat the oven to 325°F. Put eight ½-cup ramekins in a large baking pan and divide the huckleberries evenly among the ramekins; set aside.

Whip the egg yolks, sugar, and salt in an electric mixer at medium speed until well blended. Warm the whipping cream in a small saucepan over medium heat until it just reaches a low simmer. With the mixer at low speed, slowly

add the warm cream to the egg yolk mixture. Add the vanilla and continue mixing until evenly blended.

Ladle the custard into the ramekins and add boiling water to the larger baking dish to come about halfway up the sides of the ramekins. Bake until the custards are just barely set, about 25 minutes (up to 35 minutes for deep ramekins). The custards will be done when a knife inserted in the center comes out clean. Take the pan from the oven and let the custards cool to room temperature in the water bath. Take them from the water, cover with plastic wrap, and refrigerate until fully chilled, up to a day before serving.

Just before serving, evenly sprinkle 1 to 1½ teaspoons of granulated sugar over each custard. Use a blowtorch to caramelize the sugar, drawing the flame slowly and evenly over the surface until the sugar bubbles and turns a rich brown. Alternatively, caramelize the custards under the broiler, but watch carefully to avoid burning.

Let the crème brûlées cool for a minute. Top each with a dollop of unsweetened whipped cream, a scattering of huckleberries, and a sprig of mint. Serve right away.

Makes 8 servings

Triple Layer Chocolate Martini

DIVA AT THE MET, VANCOUVER, BRITISH COLUMBIA

Not a martini for sipping, this is instead a layering of rich mousses served stylishly in a martini glass. Thomas Haas, pastry chef and chocolatier for Diva at the Met, created this dessert for those with a passion for chocolate: velvety dark, white, and milk chocolate. These chocolate martinis can be made a day in advance and refrigerated, covered with plastic wrap. At Diva, they serve this dessert with a Grand Marnier—flavored crème anglaise sauce.

Dark Chocolate Cream

2 ounces top-quality bittersweet chocolate, finely chopped

6 tablespoons whipping cream

2½ tablespoons lukewarm 2% milk

White Chocolate Cream

4 ounces top-quality white chocolate, finely chopped

6 tablespoons whipping cream

2½ tablespoons lukewarm 2% milk

Milk Chocolate Cream

6½ ounces top-quality milk chocolate, finely chopped

½ cup plus 2½ tablespoons whipping cream

6 tablespoons lukewarm 2% milk

Chocolate Curls, for garnish (optional, see page 12)

For the dark chocolate cream, put the bittersweet chocolate in the top of a double boiler or in a heatproof bowl set over a pan of simmering (not boiling) water until partially melted, stirring occasionally. Take the bowl from the saucepan and continue stirring until the chocolate is melted and smooth.

Whip the cream until soft peaks form and set aside. Add the lukewarm milk, all at once, to the melted chocolate and stir with a rubber spatula (not a whisk) until blended. Add the whipped cream, all at once, and stir with a spatula until blended (the mixture will be runny). Pour one quarter of the chocolate mixture into each of 4 large (8-ounce) martini glasses. Refrigerate the glasses until the mixture is set, 30 to 40 minutes.

Once the dark chocolate cream has set, use the same method to prepare the white chocolate cream and spoon it over the dark chocolate cream in each martini glass. Refrigerate until set, about 1½ hours.

Once the white chocolate layer has set, use the same method to prepare the milk chocolate cream and spoon it over the white chocolate layer in each martini glass. Refrigerate until set, about 1½ hours.

To serve, top each glass with a few curls of chocolate (if using), set the glasses on a small plate, and serve.

Makes 4 servings

Chocolate and Brandied Dried-Cherry Bread Pudding

CAPRIAL'S BISTRO, PORTLAND, OREGON

*H*ere's an interesting twist on classic bread pudding, with chocolate added to the custard and brandy-soaked dried cherries used instead of raisins. The hard sauce, a traditional accompaniment to bread pudding, is an optional embellishment to this already-rich dessert.

1 cup dried sour cherries

1 cup brandy

1⅓ cups plus ½ cup whipping cream

1⅓ cups milk

1 vanilla bean, split lengthwise

8 ounces top-quality bittersweet chocolate, chopped

6 egg yolks

½ cup granulated sugar

6 cups cubed artisan bread

Hard Sauce (optional)

1 cup powdered sugar

½ cup unsalted butter, cut into small pieces

1 egg yolk

¼ cup brandy

For the hard sauce, if using, combine the powdered sugar and butter in the top of a double boiler or in a heatproof bowl set over a pan of simmering (not boiling) water. Heat until the butter is melted, stirring to make a smooth mixture. Whisk in the egg yolk and continue to cook until warm and lightly thickened, 3 to 5 minutes. Remove the bowl from the heat, whisk in the brandy, and mix well. Set aside to cool. Refrigerate, covered, until ready to serve. (The sauce will keep, refrigerated, for up to 1 week.)

Combine the dried cherries and brandy in a medium bowl and set aside to soak for at least 2 hours.

Preheat the oven to 300°F.

Put 1⅓ cups of the cream, the milk, and vanilla bean in a medium saucepan over medium heat and bring just to a boil. Take the pan from the heat, add the chocolate, and let stand until the chocolate is melted, 4 to 5 minutes. Whisk until smooth.

Whisk together the egg yolks and sugar in a large bowl. Slowly whisk about a cup of the hot chocolate mixture into the egg yolk mixture to bring it up to the same temperature as the chocolate. Whisk in the remaining chocolate mixture and strain it through a fine sieve. Scrape the seeds from the inside of the vanilla bean into the strained mixture and discard the bean.

Divide the bread among six 1-cup ramekins. Divide the soaked cherries and the brandy among the ramekins. Pour the custard over the bread and cherries to completely cover them. Let sit for 5 to 10 minutes, occasionally pushing the bread down gently so it will soak up the custard. Put the ramekins in a roasting pan and set the pan on the oven rack. Carefully add enough hot water to the pan to reach about halfway up the sides of the ramekins. Bake just until the custard is set, about 1 hour. To test, press gently in the center

of one of the puddings; if any custard comes up around the edges, cook them a bit longer. When cooked, take the ramekins from the water bath and let them cool on a wire rack for 15 minutes before serving. Meanwhile, whip the remaining ½ cup whipping cream to soft peaks.

Gently warm the hard sauce, if using, in a small heavy saucepan over low heat. Drizzle some of the warm sauce over the bread puddings, top with a dollop of whipped cream, and serve right away.

MAKES 6 SERVINGS

The Floating Diva

This signature drink is a colorful three-layered beverage that was created by bartender Simon Ogden and first served as a cocktail for the cast of a local play. The cocktail was so well received at the production's wrap party at the restaurant that it launched the drink's ongoing popularity in Vancouver.

1½ fluid ounces (3 tablespoons) freshly squeezed lime juice

1 fluid ounce (2 tablespoons) vodka

¾ ounce (1½ tablespoons) melon liqueur

1 fluid ounce (2 tablespoons) blue curaçao

1½ ounces (3 tablespoons) cranberry juice

Fill a large martini glass with ice and set aside to chill.

Half-fill a cocktail shaker with ice and add the lime juice, vodka, and melon liqueur. Cover and shake vigorously until well chilled. Discard the ice from the martini glass and strain the vodka mixture into the chilled glass. Drizzle the blue curaçao slowly down the side of the glass to create the bottom layer. Slowly drizzle the cranberry juice down the side of the glass to create the middle layer. Serve right away.

MAKES 1 SERVING

Coconut Crème Caramel

MONSOON, SEATTLE, WASHINGTON

A fter the vibrant flavors in the Vietnamese dishes prepared by the brother-sister team of Eric and Sophie Banh at Monsoon, it makes good sense to cap off the meal with a rich but delicately flavored dessert such as this. The addition of coconut milk to the custard hints at swaying palms on some balmy coast far away. It's important to stir up the can of coconut milk before measuring, so that you get a blend of the thicker solids with the thinner liquid.

5 egg yolks

½ cup sugar

1½ cups whipping cream

½ cup unsweetened coconut milk

Caramel

¾ cup sugar

¼ cup water

Preheat the oven to 300°F.

For the caramel, combine the sugar and water in a medium saucepan over medium heat. Stir until the sugar is dissolved, then increase the heat to medium-high, bring to a boil, and cook without stirring until the sugar caramelizes to a deep golden brown. Immediately but carefully pour the caramel into six ½-cup ramekins (note that the ramekins will quickly become very hot). Set aside to cool.

Whisk together the egg yolks and sugar in a large bowl until well blended. Add the cream and coconut milk and whisk to mix evenly. Strain the mixture through a fine sieve into a pitcher or lipped measuring cup, then pour the custard over the cooled caramel in the ramekins. Put the ramekins in a baking dish and add enough hot water to the dish to come halfway up the sides of the ramekins. Cover the dish snugly with foil and bake until the custard is set (a knife inserted in the center will come out clean), about 1 hour 15 minutes. Take the ramekins from the pan of water and set aside to cool on a wire rack. Refrigerate the cooled custards, covered with plastic wrap, until fully chilled, at least 1 hour.

To serve, set a small serving plate on top of each ramekin. Holding the two together, quickly flip them over so that the crème caramel falls onto the plate. Lift up the ramekin, holding it for a few moments to allow the caramel to drip down, and serve.

Makes 6 servings

Basil Panna Cotta with Strawberries

DAHLIA LOUNGE, SEATTLE, WASHINGTON

*P*anna cotta (which translates as "cooked cream") is an eggless Italian custard set with gelatin. A deliciously subtle infusion of fresh basil makes this panna cotta an ideal companion to our short-seasoned but intensely flavorful local strawberries. At the Dahlia Lounge, they serve this with pine nut langues du chat cookies, but you can serve it with any thin, crisp cookies. If you prefer, you can serve the panna cotta in the cup, instead of unmolding it, in which case you won't need to oil the molds.

1½ cups whipping cream

¾ cup milk

7½ tablespoons sugar, or to taste

10 large fresh basil leaves, plus small leaves for garnish

1½ teaspoons unflavored gelatin powder

2 tablespoons cold water

1 pint strawberries

Sugar cookies or shortbread, for serving

Spray the interiors of 6 demitasse cups or 4-ounce ramekins with a flavorless nonstick spray or rub them lightly with vegetable oil; set aside.

Combine the cream, milk, 5½ tablespoons of the sugar, and large basil leaves in a small saucepan. Bring the mixture to a simmer over medium heat, stirring occasionally to help the sugar dissolve. Take the pan from the heat, cover, and let sit 30 minutes. Meanwhile, sprinkle the gelatin over the cold water in a small dish and set aside to soften, about 5 minutes.

Lift the basil leaves from the cream and discard them. Add the softened gelatin to the pan and bring back to a low simmer, stirring, until the gelatin is dissolved. Pour the cream into the prepared dishes, dividing it evenly. (To make it easier to pour, you can first transfer the cream mixture to a lipped measuring cup.) Let cool to room temperature, then cover the panna cotta with plastic wrap and refrigerate until fully set, at least 4 hours.

When you are ready to serve the panna cotta, slice the strawberries and toss them in a medium bowl with about 2 tablespoons of sugar, or to your taste. Transfer ½ cup of the strawberries to a blender or food processor and purée. Stir the purée back into the sliced berries.

To serve, run a sharp knife around the edge of the panna cotta. Set a dessert plate upside down over the panna cotta, quickly flip both together, giving a quick shake or two, then lift off the dish. Spoon some of the strawberries around each panna cotta, garnish with basil leaves, and serve with cookies alongside.

Makes 6 servings

Maple, Orange, and Ginger Rice Custard

Tojo's, Vancouver, British Columbia

The warmly aromatic blend of maple, orange, and ginger makes for a compelling combination in this light Asian rice pudding. Be sure to use real maple syrup for the best results. This recipe is a great option for leftover plain steamed rice. For the candied orange-zest garnish, follow the instructions for the candied lemon zest on page 17, using a small navel orange in place of the lemon.

1¼ cups cold water

¼ teaspoon plus a pinch salt

½ cup jasmine or other long grain white rice

2 cups vanilla-flavored soy milk

1 teaspoon grated orange zest

½ cup maple syrup

1 teaspoon grated or finely minced ginger

2 teaspoons (1 envelope) unflavored gelatin powder

Orange segments, for garnish (see page 53)

Candied orange zest, for garnish (see page 17)

Black sesame seeds, for garnish

Combine 1 cup of the water and ¼ teaspoon of the salt in a small saucepan and bring to a boil over medium-high heat. Stir in the rice, cover the pan, and cook over low heat until the water is fully absorbed and the rice is tender, about 18 minutes. Fluff the rice with a fork and set aside, uncovered, to cool.

Line six ½-cup ramekins with plastic wrap.

Combine the rice, soy milk, and orange zest in a medium saucepan and bring to a boil over medium-high heat, stirring occasionally. Add the maple syrup, ginger, and remaining pinch of salt. Reduce the heat and simmer until the mixture thickens slightly, about 10 minutes. Meanwhile, sprinkle the gelatin powder over the ¼ cup of cold water in a small bowl and set aside to soften, about 5 minutes. Take the pan with the rice mixture from the heat and add the gelatin, stirring until the gelatin is melted and evenly blended with the rice. Ladle the rice mixture into the ramekins, cover with plastic wrap, and refrigerate until firm, 2 to 3 hours.

To serve, unmold the custards onto individual plates, remove the plastic wrap, and garnish with the orange segments, candied zest, and a sprinkling of sesame seeds.

Makes 6 to 8 servings

Segmenting Oranges

To cut segments from an orange so that there is no peel or membrane, start by first cutting both ends from the orange, just to the
flesh. Set the orange upright on a cutting board and use a small
sharp knife to cut away the peel and pith, following the curve of
the fruit. Try not to cut away too much of the flesh with the peel.
Working over a medium bowl to catch the juice, hold the peeled
orange in your hand and slide the knife blade down one side of a
section, cutting it from the membrane. Cut down the other side of
the same section and let it fall into the bowl. (Pick out and discard
any seeds as you go.) Continue for the remaining sections, turn-
ing the flaps of the membrane like the pages of a book. Squeeze the
juice from the membrane core into the bowl, if you need the orange
juice as well.

Use the same technique for segmenting lemons, grapefruits, and
other citrus fruits.

Tiramisu

QUATTRO ON FOURTH, VANCOUVER, BRITISH COLUMBIA

This has become a classic among desserts, a wonderful Italian tradition of coffee-soaked ladyfingers layered with a rich mascarpone mousse. If the ladyfingers you're using are soft rather than firm, you may want to arrange them in the baking dish first, then brush them with the espresso mixture. Dipping soft ladyfingers in liquid may cause them to fall apart.

⅔ cup sugar

½ cup cold water

8 egg yolks

16 ounces mascarpone

2 teaspoons (1 envelope) unflavored gelatin powder

½ cup orange liqueur or brandy

2 cups whipping cream

2 cups espresso or strong coffee

½ cup Kahlúa or other coffee-flavored liqueur

2 packages (3 ounces each) ladyfingers

Combine the sugar and ¼ cup of the water in a small saucepan and bring to a boil over medium heat, stirring often to help the sugar dissolve. Increase the heat to medium-high and cook until the sugar reaches 120°F on a candy thermometer. Meanwhile, whip the egg yolks in an electric mixer at medium-high speed until they are about double in volume and pale yellow in color. With the mixer running, slowly drizzle in the hot syrup and continue whipping until the mixture is cooled to room temperature, 5 to 10 minutes.

Gradually add the mascarpone to the egg-yolk mixture and continue beating until smooth.

Sprinkle the gelatin powder over the remaining ¼ cup of the cold water in a small bowl and set aside until softened, about 5 minutes. Put the liqueur or brandy in a small saucepan over medium–low heat. Add the gelatin and stir until melted, then whisk this into the mascarpone mixture. Whip the cream to soft peaks and fold it into the mascarpone mixture.

Combine the espresso and Kahlúa in a shallow bowl. Dip half of the ladyfingers in the espresso mixture and use them to line the bottom of a 9- by 13-inch baking dish. Spoon half of the mascarpone filling over and top with a layer of the remaining ladyfingers, dipped. Spoon the remaining mascarpone filling on top, cover with plastic, and refrigerate until set, at least 3 hours or overnight. Cut into pieces to serve.

Makes 12 to 16 servings

Bread Pudding with Plum-Port Sauce

A Touch of Europe™ Bed and Breakfast, Yakima, Washington

hile bread pudding is a standard among desserts, the dish comes in many forms. This version is particularly indulgent, rich with cream and egg yolks and imbued with brandy. When summer's fresh plums aren't available, consider making the sauce with pitted dark cherries, generally available frozen throughout the year.

6 cups whipping cream

2 cups whole milk

½ cup brandy

9 egg yolks

1½ cups sugar

20 slices white bread, crusts removed and quartered

Lightly sweetened whipped cream or vanilla ice cream, for serving (optional)

Plum-Port Sauce

1 pound fresh Italian plums, halved and pitted

¾ cup port

½ cup sugar

Preheat the oven to 325°F. Generously butter a 9- by 13-inch baking dish.

Combine the cream, milk, and brandy in a medium saucepan and heat over medium heat until quite steamy but not boiling. While this mixture is heating, whisk together the egg yolks and sugar in a large bowl until thick and creamy. Slowly add the hot cream mixture to the egg mixture, whisking constantly.

Arrange the bread pieces so they are slightly overlapping in the baking dish and pour the egg and cream mixture slowly over, submerging the bread with the back of a spoon to help it soak up the liquid. Put the dish in larger baking pan and add enough hot water to the pan so that it comes halfway up the sides. Bake the bread pudding until it is nicely puffed, the custard is set, and the top is browned, about 1 hour. The pudding will set as it cools slightly.

While the pudding is baking, make the sauce. Purée the plums, port, and sugar in a food processor until smooth. Transfer the mixture to a medium saucepan and cook over medium heat until slightly thickened, 20 to 30 minutes.

To serve, spoon a few tablespoons of the plum-port sauce onto each plate, and set a piece of warm bread pudding on top. Top with a dollop of whipped cream or a scoop of ice cream, if you like, and pass the extra sauce separately.

Makes 12 to 15 servings

Fruit & Nuts

Summer Berry Shortcake

CANLIS, SEATTLE, WASHINGTON

his is an elegant rendition of a classic summertime treat. In place of whipped cream, the bright fruit and freshly baked biscuits are layered with a rich, fluffy white chocolate ganache. A drizzle of balsamic–port reduction helps make this truly special.

I quart fresh berries (about I pound), brushed clean
(if using strawberries, quarter them)

6 large strawberries, for garnish

6 mint leaves, for garnish

White Chocolate Ganache

2 ounces top-quality white chocolate, chopped

2 cups whipping cream

Biscuits

2½ cups all-purpose flour

4 teaspoons sugar, plus more for sprinkling

I teaspoon salt

I teaspoon baking powder

½ teaspoon baking soda

6 tablespoons unsalted butter, cut into small pieces and chilled

I½ cups whipping cream, plus more for brushing

¼ cup sour cream

Balsamic–Port Reduction

2 cups tawny port

½ cup balsamic vinegar

½ cup sugar

For the white chocolate ganache, put the chocolate in a medium heatproof bowl. Heat the cream in a small saucepan over medium heat to just below the boil, pour it over the chocolate, and whisk until the chocolate is melted and the mixture is smooth. Transfer the ganache to a shallow dish and chill at least a few hours or overnight. It is important that the ganache be very cold.

For the biscuits, stir together the flour, sugar, salt, baking powder, and baking soda in an electric mixer fitted with the paddle attachment. Add the butter and mix until it has the consistency of coarse crumbs. Add the whipping cream and sour cream and mix just until combined. The dough will be slightly wet and sticky. Cover the bowl with plastic wrap and chill until the dough is firm and cold, at least 1 hour and up to 4 hours.

While the dough is chilling, make the reduction. Combine the port, vinegar, and sugar in a medium saucepan over medium heat and stir until the sugar is completely dissolved. Increase the heat to medium-high and bring the mixture to a boil, then return the heat to medium and simmer until the sauce has the consistency of thin syrup, 25 to 30 minutes. Set aside to cool.

Preheat the oven to 425°F. Lightly butter a heavy baking sheet.

When the biscuit dough has chilled, turn it out onto a floured surface and knead gently 3 or 4 times, then press it into a 6- by 9-inch rectangle about 1 inch thick. Cut the dough into 6 squares, brush the tops with cream, and

sprinkle them lightly with sugar. Transfer the biscuits to the prepared baking sheet and bake until nicely puffed and lightly browned, 17 to 20 minutes.

While the biscuits are baking, whip the cold ganache with an electric mixer at medium-high speed until stiff peaks form. Refrigerate until ready to serve.

Take the biscuits from the oven and let cool on a wire rack. Cut each biscuit in half horizontally, set the bottoms on individual plates, and top with a generous dollop of the white chocolate ganache. Put the berries in a medium bowl, drizzle with ¼ cup of the balsamic–port reduction, and toss gently to mix. Spoon the berries over the ganache and top with the remaining biscuit halves, drizzling the remaining reduction around the shortcakes. To garnish, cut each whole strawberry into thin slices, leaving them attached at the stem end, and gently press each one flat to fan it out. Set the strawberries on top of the shortcakes, tuck in a mint leaf, and serve right away.

MAKES 6 SERVINGS

Almond Pear Clafouti

CHANTICLEER INN, ASHLAND, OREGON

*T*his clafouti is an adaptation of a French classic, featuring one of the things for which the Rogue Valley is most famous: pears. You can peel the pears or not, depending on your taste, but if they have a lovely russet-colored skin it will make for a nice color contrast in the finished dish. Be sure to use ripe, juicy pears for the most flavorful results.

½ cup whole blanched almonds

⅓ cup all-purpose flour

3 eggs

1 cup milk or half-and-half

½ cup sugar

1 teaspoon vanilla extract

1 teaspoon almond extract

2 to 3 ripe pears, halved, cored, each half quartered lengthwise

Preheat the oven to 325°F. Lightly butter a 12-inch oval gratin dish or other shallow 1½-quart baking dish.

Grind the almonds in a food processor with 1 tablespoon of the flour, pulsing until the almonds are finely ground. Add the eggs, milk, sugar, remaining flour, vanilla, and almond extract and blend well, scraping the sides as needed to ensure that all the flour is incorporated.

Arrange the pear wedges evenly over the bottom of the baking dish and slowly pour the batter into the dish. Bake until puffy and golden, about 45 minutes. Serve either warm (not hot), at room temperature, or chilled, scooping the clafouti onto individual plates.

MAKES 6 SERVINGS

Wildflower Honey–Roasted Strawberries with Fennel Seed Blinis

WEST, VANCOUVER, BRITISH COLUMBIA

P astry chef Rhonda Viani serves this wonderfully aromatic dessert with a scoop of her Star Anise Ice Cream (page 153), but if you're in the market for a shortcut you could use top-quality vanilla bean ice cream instead. The roasted strawberries and blinis will be at their best if made just before serving. For a fall treat, this recipe would also be tasty with roasted figs, trimmed and quartered before roasting.

1 pound fresh strawberries, stems removed

¼ cup wildflower honey

¼ vanilla bean, split lengthwise

Fennel Seed Blinis

2 eggs, separated

1 cup milk

¾ cup all-purpose flour

1 teaspoon baking powder

¼ cup sour cream

1 teaspoon ground fennel seeds

2 tablespoons sugar

Pinch salt

2 tablespoons melted unsalted butter, cooled, plus more for cooking blinis

Preheat the oven to 375°F.

Put the strawberries in a baking dish large enough to hold them in a single layer. Drizzle the honey over and nestle the vanilla bean underneath the strawberries to prevent it from drying out. Roast the strawberries until they are hot and the juices are beginning to mix with the honey, about 15 minutes, stirring gently a few times to ensure the strawberries are well coated in honey and are roasting evenly.

While the strawberries are roasting, make the blinis. Combine the egg yolks and milk in a medium bowl and whisk to mix. Sift together the flour and baking powder into another bowl, then slowly stir the flour into the milk mixture. Stir in the sour cream and fennel seeds. Whip together the egg whites, sugar, and salt in an electric mixer at medium-high speed until stiff peaks form. Fold the egg whites into the batter until evenly blended. Fold in the melted butter.

Heat a thin coating of butter in a large nonstick skillet over medium heat. Form blinis of about 2 tablespoons each and cook until bubbles appear on the surface and the bottom is lightly browned, 2 to 3 minutes. Flip the blinis over and cook until the bottom is browned, about 2 minutes longer. Arrange the blinis on a plate and continue cooking the rest of the blinis (you should have about 24 blinis total).

To serve, arrange four blinis, slightly overlapping, on six individual plates. Spoon the roasted strawberries and their cooking liquids over the blinis and serve right away.

MAKES 6 SERVINGS

Hazelnut Torte

BEDDIS HOUSE BED AND BREAKFAST, SALT SPRING ISLAND, BRITISH COLUMBIA

This is a surprisingly no-fuss cake recipe. The batter is simply whirled together in the blender, poured into prepared cake pans, and baked. What could be easier? A blender will chop the nuts more finely, though in a pinch you could use a food processor, being careful to work the batter well to create a smooth texture.

4 eggs

¾ cup granulated sugar

1 cup toasted skinned hazelnuts (see page 68)

2 tablespoons all-purpose flour or cornstarch

2½ teaspoons baking powder

Mocha Filling

1 cup powdered sugar

2 tablespoons unsalted butter, at room temperature

2 tablespoons espresso or very strong coffee, at room temperature

1 teaspoon unsweetened cocoa powder

½ teaspoon vanilla extract

Frosting

1 cup whipping cream

2 tablespoons powdered sugar

Preheat the oven to 350°F. Butter two 8-inch cake pans and line them with parchment paper.

Combine the eggs and granulated sugar in a blender and blend until smooth. Add the hazelnuts, flour, and baking powder and blend at high speed until the hazelnuts are finely ground and the batter is smooth. Pour the batter into the prepared pans and bake until a toothpick inserted in the center comes out clean, about 20 minutes. Let cool completely on a wire rack. Unmold and peel away the paper.

For the mocha filling, cream together the powdered sugar and butter in a medium bowl with a wooden spoon until smooth. Stir in the coffee, cocoa powder, and vanilla. Chill briefly to thicken. Set a layer of the cake on a serving plate, spread the filling over, and top with the second cake layer.

For the frosting, whip the cream to medium peaks, add the powdered sugar, and continue whipping to stiff peaks. Spread the whipped cream over the top and sides of the cake. Serve right away.

Makes 8 servings

Toasting Nuts

Toasting nuts does wonders for bringing out their aroma and flavor before adding them to a recipe. In the case of hazelnuts, toasting also helps remove the skin, which has a slightly bitter flavor to it.

To toast nuts, preheat the oven to 350°F. Scatter the nuts in a baking pan and toast in the oven until lightly browned and aromatic, about 4 to 5 minutes for small or sliced nuts, 8 to 10 minutes for hazelnuts and almonds. Shake the pan gently once or twice to help the nuts toast evenly. For hazelnuts, transfer them directly to a lightly dampened dishcloth and wrap the towel up around the nuts. Let sit until almost fully cooled, then rub the nuts in the cloth to help remove the papery skin. Don't worry about removing every last bit of skin; just get as much as you can. Let the hazelnuts cool completely before continuing.

Marionberry Phyllo

T he marionberry is a variety of blackberry that was developed in Marion County, Oregon, in the 1950s. Regular blackberries or other berries such as loganberries or raspberries could be used in place of the marionberries. Any remaining berry juice from the filling will be delicious spooned over the vanilla ice cream alongside, if you are using it. Individually frozen berries, rather than those frozen in syrup, can be used in place of fresh berries when they are out of season.

Phyllo has recently become available in sheets half the size of traditional phyllo sheets (9 by 14 inches compared to 14 by 18 inches). If the sheets you buy are the smaller type, layer two sheets with butter and continue as directed for the larger sheet folded in half.

1 quart fresh marionberries (about 1 pound)

½ cup granulated sugar, or more to taste

¼ cup blackberry liqueur

2 tablespoons cornstarch dissolved in 2 tablespoons water

1 package phyllo dough

1 cup unsalted butter, melted

Powdered sugar, for serving

Vanilla ice cream, for serving (optional)

Combine the berries, sugar, and liqueur in a medium saucepan over medium-high heat. Bring just to a low boil, gently stir in the cornstarch mixture, and continue simmering until the berry mixture is thickened, 2 to 3 minutes, stirring gently to avoid breaking up the berries. Taste the filling, adding a bit more sugar if needed to suit your taste. Set aside to cool for a few minutes; the filling will become juicier the longer it sits.

Preheat the oven to 400°F. Line 2 baking sheets with parchment paper or silicone baking mats or grease the baking sheets.

Open the package of phyllo dough and lay the sheets out flat on a clean work surface. Cover the phyllo with a large piece of plastic wrap, and cover the plastic wrap with a lightly damp dishtowel. Make sure the melted butter is just warm, not hot. Carefully lift the top sheet of phyllo from the pile and lay it horizontally on a clean work surface (re-cover the remaining sheets). Use a pastry brush to lightly butter the full surface of the phyllo sheet and then fold it in half crosswise. Lightly butter the surface again. Spoon a generous tablespoon of the berry filling (more berries than juice) about 2 inches up from the bottom edge of the phyllo dough, centered on the sheet. Fold the bottom edge up to cover the filling, then evenly fold in both long sides to partly cover the filling. Lightly butter the pastry strip and fold the filling upwards along the strip to form a squarish packet. Don't form too tight a packet or it will burst during cooking; work loosely to allow for expansion. Set the phyllo packet seam side down on a prepared baking sheet, lay a dishtowel over it to keep it from drying out, and continue with the remaining berry filling (you should end up with about 18 packets).

When all of the berry packets have been made, lightly brush the tops with melted butter. Bake until the pastry is crisp and well browned, about 20 minutes. Dust the phyllo packets with powdered sugar and arrange on individual plates for serving, with a scoop of vanilla ice cream alongside if you like.

Makes 6 to 8 servings

Braeburn Apples with a Walnut Filling Baked in Pommeau

HIGGINS RESTAURANT AND BAR, PORTLAND, OREGON

The kitchen fills with wonderful aromas while these apples bake, and wafts of maple, nuts, cinnamon, and apple essence whet your appetite for this rustic dessert. Pastry chef Faith Christner bakes the apples with pommeau, a traditional French blend of fresh cider with apple brandy that is aged before bottling. She uses White Oak Cider's pommeau from Newberg, Oregon, available in select stores in the Northwest. If you use the cider–brandy alternative, an ideal brandy choice would be the apple brandy produced by Portland's Clear Creek Distillery.

6 Braeburn apples or your favorite baking apple

½ cup whipping cream

¼ cup sugar

I egg

¼ cup maple syrup

½ teaspoon vanilla extract

¼ teaspoon ground cinnamon

⅛ teaspoon salt

⅔ cup walnuts, toasted and chopped

I cup White Oak Cider pommeau or ¾ cup fresh apple cider and ¼ cup apple brandy

Vanilla ice cream, for serving

Preheat the oven to 375°F.

Cut away a thin slice from the base of the apples so that they stand steady. Working from the stem end of the apple, use a melon baller or a small spoon to carefully remove the seeds and some of the flesh from the center to make room for the filling. Be careful not to go through the base of the apple or the filling will run out.

Bring the cream and sugar to a boil in a small saucepan over medium-high heat. In a small bowl, whisk together the egg, maple syrup, vanilla, cinnamon, and salt. Gradually whisk the hot cream into the egg mixture. Add the walnuts and spoon the filling into the cavities of the apples.

Pour the pommeau or cider and apple brandy into a shallow baking pan and stand the apples in the pan so that they aren't touching. Bake until the apples are tender and the custard is set, about 1 hour. Set the pan aside on a wire rack to cool slightly, 15 to 20 minutes. Serve warm on individual plates with the pan juices drizzled over and a scoop of vanilla ice cream alongside.

MAKES 6 SERVINGS

Apricot Cake

DURLACHER HOF, WHISTLER, BRITISH COLUMBIA

This traditional European apricot cake is an all-time favorite in every Austrian household," notes innkeeper Erika Durlacher. It is a rustic but pretty dessert that makes the most of summer's fresh apricots, although other soft fruits such as peaches or blackberries may be used in their place. You could also use cottage cheese in place of the ricotta cheese, if you prefer.

1½ pounds fresh apricots

1½ cups ricotta cheese

2 eggs, lightly beaten

3 tablespoons sugar

2 tablespoons cornstarch

Grated zest and juice of ½ lemon

3 tablespoons sliced almonds

Lightly sweetened whipped cream, for serving (optional)

Yeast Dough

½ cup warm milk (about 110°F)

1 tablespoon sugar

2 teaspoons (1 envelope) active dry yeast

1½ cups all-purpose flour

3 tablespoons unsalted butter, melted and cooled slightly

½ lightly beaten egg

For the dough, put the warm milk in a small bowl, stir in a pinch of the sugar, and sprinkle the yeast over the top. Set aside until frothy, about 5 minutes. Sift the flour and remaining sugar into a large bowl. Lightly whisk the butter and egg into the yeast mixture and pour it into the dry ingredients, stirring to form a smooth dough. Turn the dough out onto a lightly floured work surface and knead for 5 minutes. Put the dough in a large bowl, cover with a dishtowel, and let rise in a warm place until generously doubled in bulk, about 30 minutes.

Preheat the oven to 425°F. Lightly butter a 9- by 13-inch baking dish.

Rinse, halve, and pit the apricots. Set aside. Stir together the ricotta cheese, eggs, sugar, cornstarch, and lemon zest and juice in a small bowl. Set aside.

Roll out the risen dough on a lightly floured work surface to a rectangle just a bit larger than the baking dish, then transfer the dough to the dish and press up the edges about ¾ inch all the way around. Spread the ricotta cheese mixture over the dough and arrange the apricots cut side down on top. Sprinkle the sliced almonds evenly over and bake until the dough is nicely browned and the cheese filling is set, about 30 minutes. Let cool slightly on a wire rack. Cut into squares and serve with whipped cream, if desired.

Makes 12 to 15 servings

Raspberry Hazelnut Meringue

JACKSONVILLE INN, JACKSONVILLE, OREGON

Hazelnuts add wonderful texture and flavor to light, airy meringues, layered here with a simple whipped cream—fresh raspberry filling. Other fresh fruits could be used in place of the raspberries, including juicy fresh peaches or nectarines, coarsely chopped.

3 egg whites

Pinch cream of tartar

1 cup granulated sugar

½ cup finely ground toasted hazelnuts

Powdered sugar, for garnish

Filling

1½ cups whipping cream

⅓ cup powdered sugar

½ teaspoon vanilla extract

3 cups fresh raspberries

Preheat the oven to 225°F. Line a large baking sheet with parchment paper.

Whip together the egg whites and the cream of tartar in an electric mixer at medium-high speed until frothy. Slowly add the sugar and continue beating until the sugar is dissolved and the egg whites are glossy and thick. Gently fold in the ground hazelnuts with a rubber spatula.

Form 8 circles of meringue, each about 4 inches across, on the prepared pan, smoothing the tops so they are even. Bake until fully dried and light golden,

about 2 hours. Take the meringues from the oven and let cool in the pan on a wire rack.

For the filling, whip together the cream, sugar, and vanilla in an electric mixer at medium-high speed until stiff. Fold in the raspberries.

Gently peel the meringues away from the parchment paper. Set 4 meringues on individual plates and top with a generous layer of the raspberry filling. Put the remaining meringue disks on top, dust with powdered sugar, and serve.

Makes 4 servings

Apple-Cranberry Pudding
with Caramel Sauce

TURTLEBACK FARM INN, ORCAS ISLAND, WASHINGTON

*S*weet apples and tart cranberries pair up perfectly in this baked dessert that's a fresh take on a classic fruit crisp. If the apples you're using are quite tart, you may want to increase the amount of granulated sugar by a few tablespoons.

4 large baking apples, peeled, cored, and cut into ¼-inch slices

1 cup whole fresh cranberries

1 cup all-purpose flour

½ cup granulated sugar

½ cup packed light brown sugar

1 teaspoon baking powder

½ teaspoon salt

1 egg, beaten

4 tablespoons unsalted butter, cut into small pieces

½ teaspoon ground cinnamon

¼ cup water

Lightly sweetened whipped cream or vanilla ice cream, for serving

Caramel Sauce

1½ cups packed light brown sugar

½ cup unsalted butter

½ cup whipping cream

Preheat the oven to 375°F. Generously butter a 9- by 11-inch baking dish or other 2-quart shallow baking dish.

Put the apple slices in the prepared baking dish and scatter the cranberries evenly over the apples. Stir together the flour, granulated sugar, brown sugar, baking powder, and salt in a medium bowl. Stir in the beaten egg until well mixed. (The mixture will be dry and crumbly.) Sprinkle the mixture evenly over the apples and cranberries. Scatter the butter pieces over the top of the pudding. Dust the topping with the cinnamon. Pour the water in along the edge of the pan. Bake until the apples are tender when pierced with a fork, about 50 minutes.

For the caramel sauce, slowly melt the brown sugar and butter together in a medium saucepan over medium heat, stirring often. Whisk in the cream until the sugar has dissolved and the sauce is smooth, 3 to 4 minutes. Be careful not to scorch the sauce.

Serve the pudding warm with warm caramel sauce and whipped cream or ice cream.

Makes 6 to 8 servings

Roasted Pears with Szechwan Pepper and Bittersweet Chocolate Sauce

THE AERIE, MALAHAT, BRITISH COLUMBIA

The peppery essence of these poached pears is an unexpected—but delightful—contrast to the sweetness of the fruit and the richness of the chocolate sauce. Accompanying the pears is a striking tower of crisp pastry (also embellished with pepper) and mango sorbet, though you can omit this to streamline the recipe if you wish. As this book goes to press, a ban on importing whole Szechwan peppercorns into the United States is still in place, though the spice is available in Canada. If you are unable to find Szechwan peppercorns, you can use 1 tablespoon of coarsely ground black peppercorns in their place.

4 cups water

3 cups granulated sugar

1½ tablespoons Szechwan peppercorns, lightly toasted and ground

1 vanilla bean, split lengthwise

4 small ripe but firm pears

Fresh mint sprigs, for garnish

Mango Sorbet

1 large ripe mango, peeled, pitted, and chopped

1 cup granulated sugar

1 cup water

¼ cup honey

Bittersweet Chocolate Sauce

4½ ounces top-quality bittersweet chocolate, chopped

½ cup water

⅓ cup granulated sugar

⅓ cup unsweetened cocoa powder

¼ cup whipping cream

Spiced Craquelin

1 cup powdered sugar

1½ teaspoons freshly ground black pepper

1 sheet puff pastry

For the mango sorbet, purée the mango in a food processor until very smooth. Press the mango through a medium sieve to remove the stringy bits and set the purée aside. Combine the sugar, water, and honey in a large saucepan and bring to a boil over medium-high heat, stirring occasionally to help the sugar and honey dissolve. Reduce the heat to low and simmer gently for 15 minutes. Take the pan from the heat and let cool to room temperature. Whisk the syrup into the mango purée until evenly blended. Refrigerate until fully chilled. Pour the mixture into an ice cream maker and freeze according to the manufacturer's instructions. Transfer the ice cream to an airtight container and freeze until set, at least 2 hours.

For the poached pears, bring the water, sugar, Szechwan pepper, and vanilla bean to a boil in a medium saucepan over medium-high heat, stirring occasionally until the sugar dissolves. Reduce the heat to medium, and simmer for 30 minutes to infuse the syrup and reduce the liquid slightly.

Peel the pears and core them from the bottom, using a small spoon or melon baller to remove the core while leaving the pear whole. Add the pears to the syrup. Cut a round of parchment paper the same diameter as the pan and lay the paper directly on top of the pears. Poach the pears until they are just tender when pierced with the tip of a knife, about 10 minutes. Take the pan from the heat and let the pears cool in the syrup.

For the chocolate sauce, combine the chocolate, water, sugar, cocoa powder, and cream in a small saucepan and bring just to a low boil over medium-high heat, whisking often. Reduce the heat to medium-low and simmer for 5 minutes, whisking often. Take the pan from the heat and let the sauce cool to room temperature.

Preheat the oven to 375°F. Line a baking sheet with parchment paper or a silicone baking mat.

For the spiced craquelin, stir together the powdered sugar and pepper in a small bowl. Dust a clean work surface with the mixture and roll out the puff pastry to as near paper thickness as possible; roll the dough with moderate strokes, alternating directions to maintain the shape and adding more sugar mixture to the work surface or the top of the dough as needed to avoid sticking. Cut the pastry into triangles 3 inches long, measured from point to point, and put them on the prepared baking sheet. Bake until golden brown, about 10 minutes. Let the triangles cool completely on the baking sheet. Remove the triangles with a spatula to avoid breaking the tips.

Increase the oven temperature to 500°F and set the oven rack at the lowest level. Set the pears upright in a lightly oiled shallow baking dish and roast on the bottom rack of the oven until lightly browned on the outside, 5 to 10 minutes.

To serve, spoon a small pool of chocolate sauce to one side of each large dessert plate and set a pear upright on the sauce. Build a small tower of craquelin and mango sorbet alongside: Set a pastry triangle on the plate, top with a small scoop of sorbet, add another triangle and another scoop of sorbet, finishing with a third craquelin. Garnish with fresh mint and serve right away.

MAKES 4 SERVINGS

Golden Pineapple Carpaccio with Coriander Sugar and Lime Sorbet

DIVA AT THE MET, VANCOUVER, BRITISH COLUMBIA

his signature dessert from celebrated Vancouver pastry chef Thomas Haas is a sure crowd pleaser for summer dinner parties, a simple, refreshing, and tangy finish to the meal. For the coriander sugar, it is very important that the herb leaves (also known as cilantro) be totally dry before blending with the sugar. If there is water still clinging to the leaves, the sugar may dissolve rather than remaining granular.

40 coriander (cilantro) leaves, rinsed and very well dried

1 cup granulated sugar

2 to 3 vanilla beans, split lengthwise and seeds scraped out

1 large ripe pineapple

2 tablespoons powdered sugar

Lime Sorbet

½ cup sugar

½ cup water

⅔ cup whole milk

⅔ cup freshly squeezed lime juice (about 5 limes)

Grated zest of 2 limes

For the lime sorbet, combine the sugar and water in a small saucepan and cook over medium heat just until the sugar is dissolved, stirring occasionally. Set aside to cool. When the syrup is cool, add the milk, lime juice, and lime

zest. Refrigerate the mixture until fully chilled. Pour the sorbet base into an ice cream maker and freeze according to the manufacturer's instructions. Transfer the sorbet to an airtight container and freeze until set, at least 2 hours.

Preheat the oven to 250°F. Line a baking sheet with parchment paper or a silicone baking mat.

Combine the coriander leaves and sugar in a food processor and pulse until the coriander is very finely chopped and well blended with the sugar, which will turn an even green color. Add the vanilla seeds to the sugar mixture and pulse again to blend well. Store in an airtight container until ready to serve.

Trim the ends from the pineapple and cut away the tough outer skin. Slice the pineapple into very thin slices, about 32 slices. Lay 8 of the pineapple slices on the prepared baking sheet; wrap the remaining slices in plastic and refrigerate until ready to serve. Put the 2 tablespoons powdered sugar in a small sieve and sprinkle it evenly over the pineapple slices on the baking sheet and bake until the slices are evenly golden and dried, about 1 hour (they'll crisp up more when cool). Let cool slightly on the sheet, then peel off the slices and let cool completely on a wire rack. When cool and crisp, store them in an airtight container until ready to serve.

To serve, arrange the reserved pineapple slices, slightly overlapping, on 8 individual dessert plates. Sprinkle them with the coriander sugar. Add a scoop of sorbet to the center of the plate and pose one of the crisped pine-apple slices upright in the sorbet or perched alongside. Serve right away.

MAKES 8 SERVINGS

Nectarine Cobbler

Bugatti's Ristorante, West Linn, Oregon

This aromatic cobbler would also be delicious made with peaches or with a combination of peaches and nectarines. The optional addition of fresh raspberries adds bright flavor and a splash of color to this simple summertime dessert.

2½ pounds fresh nectarines, halved, pitted, and cut into 1-inch slices

1 cup fresh raspberries (optional)

½ cup sugar, or less, depending on sweetness of the fruit

3 tablespoons freshly squeezed lemon juice

1 tablespoon cornstarch

½ teaspoon ground cinnamon

½ teaspoon powdered ginger

⅛ teaspoon almond extract

3 tablespoons unsalted butter, cut into small pieces

Topping

2 cups all-purpose flour

2 tablespoons sugar

1 tablespoon baking powder

¾ teaspoon salt

7 tablespoons unsalted butter, cut into small pieces and chilled, plus
3 tablespoons, melted

1 cup whipping cream

Preheat the oven to 400°F.

Toss together the nectarines, raspberries (if using), sugar, lemon juice, cornstarch, cinnamon, ginger, and almond extract in a large bowl. Pour the mixture into a 9- by 13-inch baking dish and dot the top with the butter. Cover the pan with foil and bake until the fruit is bubbling and half-tender, about 20 minutes. (The fruit must be bubbling or the topping will bake up doughy.)

While the fruit is cooking, make the topping. Pulse together the flour, sugar, baking powder, and salt in a food processor. Add the cold butter and pulse until the mixture resembles coarse meal (better to underblend than overblend). Transfer the mixture to a bowl and keep in the refrigerator while the fruit is baking.

When the fruit is ready, add the cream to the topping mixture and stir with 5 or 6 firm strokes. Some flour will remain unincorporated; the less mixing the better. Crumble the topping over the hot fruit, drizzle with the melted butter, and bake until the topping is golden brown and nicely puffed, about 20 minutes longer. Let cool slightly before scooping into bowls to serve.

MAKES 8 TO 12 SERVINGS

Macadamia Nut Sour Cream Cake

THE PLACE BAR AND GRILL, FRIDAY HARBOR, WASHINGTON

Thisis a variation on pound cake, but so much better with the addition of rich macadamia nuts and sour cream for moistness. At The Place, they serve this cake with fresh berries or mango coulis during the summer, for something of a twist on berry shortcake. The berries they use—including strawberries, raspberries, various types of blackberries, and blueberries—come from the Skagit Valley in Northwest Washington, a prolific berry-growing region. The cake keeps well, thanks to its richness, so you can enjoy it over the course of a few days.

To grind the macadamia nuts, pulse them in a food processor until rather fine in texture; adding a tablespoon or two of the flour while grinding the nuts will help avoid overworking them to a paste.

½ cup unsalted butter, at room temperature

1½ cups sugar

3 eggs

½ cup ground macadamia nuts

1 teaspoon vanilla extract

1½ cups all-purpose flour

⅛ teaspoon baking powder

⅛ teaspoon baking soda

½ cup sour cream

Preheat the oven to 325°F. Butter and flour a 9- by 5-inch loaf pan.

Cream the butter with an electric mixer at medium-high speed until light. Gradually add the sugar and continue beating until fluffy, about 5 minutes. Add the eggs, one at a time, mixing just until the yellow disappears, and

scraping down the sides of the bowl as needed. Stir in the ground macadamia nuts and vanilla.

In a small bowl, stir together the flour, baking powder, and baking soda. Add the dry ingredients in 3 parts to the butter mixture, alternating with the sour cream in 2 parts. Spoon the batter into the loaf pan and bake until a tooth-pick inserted in the center comes out clean, about 1 hour and 20 minutes. Rotate the pan in the oven halfway through to make sure it browns evenly. Let the cake cool on a wire rack. Turn it out onto a cutting board and cut into slices to serve.

MAKES 10 TO 12 SERVINGS

Oregon Berry Cheesecake

The Arbor Cafe, Salem, Oregon

The opening of the Farmers' Wednesday Market across the street from The Arbor Cafe, with all its splendid Oregon berries, inspired Lynne Strelow to create a cheesecake that showcased the wide array of Oregon cane berries (a family of berries that includes raspberries, blackberries, and boysenberries). This no-bake cheesecake filling can be made with any one berry type or a combination of varieties. Blueberries may also be used, but the purée must be cooked to give it a full flavor.

Berries are at their best if not washed in water, which makes them soggy. Ideally, just brush the berries clean as needed with a pastry brush or lightly dampened paper towel.

1 quart fresh berries (about 1 pound), brushed clean

1 teaspoon unflavored gelatin powder

2 tablespoons cold water

⅓ cup granulated sugar

2 teaspoons freshly squeezed lemon juice

2 pounds cream cheese, at room temperature

¾ cup plus 2 tablespoons powdered sugar

1¾ cups whipping cream

Crust

2 cups coarsely crushed vanilla wafer crumbs
(about 45 cookies or half of a 12-ounce box)

½ cup toasted skinned hazelnuts or pecans

¼ cup unsalted butter, cut into small pieces

Preheat the oven to 350°F.

For the crust, finely grind the vanilla wafers and nuts in a food processor. Add the butter and pulse until evenly mixed. Press the mixture onto the bottom of a 9- or 10-inch springform pan and bake until lightly browned and aromatic, about 10 minutes. Set aside on a wire rack to cool.

Pick over the berries to remove any stems or other debris. Purée half of the berries in a food processor or blender until very smooth. If the berries are seedy, strain them through a fine sieve, pressing to obtain as much of the purée as possible.

Sprinkle the gelatin over the cold water in a small dish and set aside until softened, about 5 minutes. Put the softened gelatin in a small saucepan and warm over low heat until melted, stirring occasionally, about 1 minute. Stir in the granulated sugar and lemon juice and cook until the sugar is dissolved, 2 to 3 minutes, stirring often. Stir in the berry purée and set aside to cool.

Beat the cream cheese and ¾ cup of the powdered sugar in an electric mixer at medium speed until smooth. Add the cooled berry and gelatin mixture and beat slowly until well blended. In a separate bowl, whip 1 cup of the cream until moderately stiff peaks form. Gently but thoroughly fold the whipped cream into the cream cheese mixture. Set aside 12 of the remaining whole berries for garnish and fold the rest into the cheesecake mixture. Pour the mixture into the cooled crust, cover with plastic, and chill until set, at least 4 hours or overnight.

To serve, run a warm knife around edge of the cake and remove the sides of the pan. Whip the remaining ¾ cup cream with the remaining 2 tablespoons powdered sugar until soft peaks form. Cut the cheesecake into wedges and top each with a dollop of whipped cream and a berry.

MAKES 12 SERVINGS

Cookies & Bars

Espresso Brownies

LINDAMAN'S GOURMET BISTRO, SPOKANE, WASHINGTON

C hocolate and coffee are a favorite combo on the dessert hit parade. Here—for the true Northwest coffee fiends out there—finely ground coffee beans are added directly to the rich brownie batter. A final flourish of glaze embellished with Baileys caps the brownies off in style.

1½ cups unsalted butter, at room temperature

5 ounces top-quality unsweetened chocolate, chopped

½ cup finely ground espresso or dark-roast coffee

½ teaspoon salt

2½ cups granulated sugar

5 eggs

2 teaspoons vanilla extract

1¼ cups all-purpose flour

1 cup pecan pieces

Baileys Glaze

¼ cup Baileys or other cream liqueur

1 tablespoon unsalted butter, at room temperature

1 teaspoon vanilla extract

1 cup powdered sugar

Chocolate Glaze

6 ounces top-quality semisweet chocolate, chopped

½ cup heavy cream

Preheat the oven to 325°F. Butter and flour a 9- or 10-inch springform pan, line the bottom with parchment paper, and butter and flour the paper.

Combine the butter, chocolate, espresso, and salt in the top of a double boiler or in a heatproof bowl set over a pan of simmering (not boiling) water. Heat the mixture until melted, stirring occasionally. Set aside to cool slightly.

Whisk together the sugar, eggs, and vanilla in a large bowl until smooth. Add the chocolate mixture and whisk until combined. Fold in the flour just until blended, then fold in the pecans. Pour the batter into the prepared pan and smooth the top. Bake until a toothpick comes out clean, about 1 hour.

For the Baileys glaze, whisk together the liqueur, butter, and vanilla until blended. Add the powdered sugar and beat until smooth. Spread the glaze over the warm brownies and let sit for at least an hour to set.

For the chocolate glaze, melt the chocolate in the top of a double boiler or in a heatproof bowl set over a pan of simmering (not boiling) water. Take the chocolate from the heat and whisk in the cream until smooth. Spread the glaze over the brownies and refrigerate until set, about 30 minutes, before cutting into wedges to serve.

Makes 12 to 16 servings

Oatmeal Chip Cookies

STRATFORD MANOR BED & BREAKFAST, BELLINGHAM, WASHINGTON

No matter how old we get, we never outgrow cookies. The aroma that spreads through the house when cookies bake is enough to soothe any weary soul. This recipe blends the nutty character of oatmeal cookies with chocolate chips, and is enhanced with flavor from molasses as well.

I cup packed light brown sugar

I cup granulated sugar

I cup vegetable shortening

2 eggs

¼ cup molasses

I teaspoon vanilla extract

I½ cups all-purpose flour

I teaspoon baking soda

3 cups quick-cooking oatmeal

I cup semisweet chocolate chips

½ cup raisins

Preheat the oven to 350°F. Lightly grease 2 baking sheets or line them with parchment paper or silicone baking mats.

Cream together the brown sugar, granulated sugar, and shortening in an electric mixer at medium speed until light and fluffy. Add the eggs, molasses, and vanilla, and mix until well blended, scraping down the sides of the bowl as needed. Add the flour and baking soda and mix together well. Stir in the oatmeal, chocolate chips, and raisins by hand with a large wooden spoon

until evenly blended. Drop the batter by generous teaspoonfuls onto the baking sheets, about 2 inches apart. Bake until nicely puffed and firm to the touch, about 10 minutes. Transfer the cookies to a wire rack to cool and continue baking the remaining cookies.

MAKES 3 DOZEN COOKIES

Triple Chocolate Brownie

THIRD FLOOR FISH CAFE, KIRKLAND, WASHINGTON

reamy vanilla ice cream would be an ideal accent for these intensely chocolate brownies. Pastry chef Sandra Watson prefers using Callebaut brand Belgian chocolate for indulgent desserts such as this one. You might also want to serve the brownies with fresh berries alongside.

6½ ounces top-quality bittersweet chocolate, finely chopped

1¼ cups plus 2 tablespoons all-purpose flour

½ teaspoon baking powder

3 ounces top-quality white chocolate, chopped into ½-inch pieces

3 ounces top-quality milk chocolate, chopped into ½-inch pieces

1 cup sugar

⅔ cup unsalted butter, at room temperature

3 eggs

½ teaspoon vanilla extract

Ganache Glaze

4 ounces top-quality bittersweet chocolate, finely chopped

½ cup whipping cream

1 tablespoon light corn syrup

Preheat the oven to 350°F. Butter a 9-inch square baking pan, dust it with flour, and tap out the excess.

For the brownies, melt the bittersweet chocolate in the top of a double boiler or in a heatproof bowl set over a pan of simmering (not boiling) water, stirring until smooth; set aside. Sift together the flour and baking powder into

a small bowl. Add the white and milk chocolate pieces, toss to coat, and set aside. Cream together the sugar and butter with an electric mixer at medium-high speed until light and fluffy. Add the eggs one at a time, mixing well and scraping down the bowl after each addition. Beat in the vanilla. Use a wooden spoon to stir in the melted chocolate, then fold in the flour-chocolate mixture until just evenly blended. Spoon the batter into the baking pan, smoothing the top. Bake until the edges begin to pull away from the sides of the pan, about 40 minutes. Let cool on a wire rack.

For the ganache glaze, put the chocolate in a heatproof bowl. Bring the cream and corn syrup to a boil in a small saucepan over medium heat. Pour the hot cream over the chocolate and stir gently with a rubber spatula until completely smooth. Set aside for 10 minutes to cool slightly.

Turn the cooled brownie out onto a serving plate. Pour the glaze over and spread it evenly to the edges so it drizzles a bit down the sides. Refrigerate to set the ganache. Cut into portions for serving.

Makes 8 to 10 servings

Pistachio-Orange Biscotti

ith a name like Bugatti's, it's little wonder that the cookie of choice at this restaurant is *the biscotti. This version of the classic Italian cookie has a wonderful nutty texture, with aroma and flavor from fresh orange zest.*

1½ cups pistachios (about 6 ounces shelled pistachios)

1¾ cups all-purpose flour

½ teaspoon baking soda

½ teaspoon baking powder

⅛ teaspoon salt

1 cup sugar

½ cup unsalted butter

2 tablespoons grated orange zest

2 eggs

1½ teaspoons vanilla extract

Preheat the oven to 350°F. Lightly grease a large baking sheet or line it with parchment paper or a silicone baking mat.

Scatter the pistachios in a baking pan and toast them in the oven until lightly browned and aromatic, 6 to 8 minutes, gently shaking the pan once or twice to help the nuts toast evenly. Let cool. Coarsely chop the pistachios and set aside. Leave the oven set at 350°F.

Sift together the flour, baking soda, baking powder, and salt and set aside. Cream together the sugar, butter, and orange zest in an electric mixer at

medium speed until light and fluffy. Add the eggs and vanilla and mix until smooth, scraping down the sides of the bowl as needed. Add the pistachios and mix to blend. Gently fold in the dry ingredients just until incorporated. (If the dough is quite soft, refrigerate for about 15 minutes before continuing.)

Working on a lightly floured work surface with lightly floured hands, form the dough into 2 logs about 2 inches wide and 1 inch thick and put them on the baking sheet. Bake until golden brown and firm, about 30 minutes. Take the pan from the oven to cool slightly on a wire rack. Reduce the oven temperature to 325°F.

Cut the biscotti logs into ½-inch slices at a slight angle, lay them on their sides on the baking pan, and bake until they are dry, about 8 minutes. Take them from the oven, turn them over, and bake until the other side is dry, about 8 minutes longer. Transfer the biscotti to a wire rack to cool completely before serving.

MAKES ABOUT 4 DOZEN BISCOTTI

Sarah Bernhardts

This classy dessert is said to have been created in Scandinavia as a tribute to the famous English tragedienne, Sarah Bernhardt. The almond macaroon base is topped with fluffy chocolate cream and a dark chocolate coating, perfect alongside an after-dinner cup of coffee. You will have leftover melted chocolate after glazing the cookies, but the quantity provides the volume needed to make dipping easy. Extra chocolate can be saved for another use. Sarah Bernhardts are best eaten the day they are made.

Almond paste can be found alongside other baking supplies, in a tube or small can.

4 ounces almond paste

⅓ cup plus 1 tablespoon sugar

1 egg white, lightly beaten

Chocolate Whipped Cream

2½ ounces top-quality bittersweet chocolate, chopped

1 cup whipping cream

Glaze

1 pound top-quality bittersweet chocolate, chopped

12 blanched almonds, lightly toasted

Preheat the oven to 350°F. Line a baking sheet with parchment paper or a silicone baking mat.

Blend the almond paste and sugar with an electric mixer fitted with the paddle attachment at medium speed until the mixture has the texture of fine meal.

Slowly add the egg white and continue mixing until the batter is smooth. Spoon into a pastry bag fitted with a medium plain tip and pipe out 12 mounds about 2 inches apart on the prepared baking sheet, making mounds about 1½ inches wide. (Alternatively, simply spoon the batter onto the baking sheet as neatly as possible.) Bake the macaroons until light golden brown, 15 to 17 minutes. Transfer the macaroons to a wire rack to cool completely.

For the chocolate cream, melt the chocolate in the top of a double boiler or in a heatproof bowl set over a pan of simmering (not boiling) water, stirring until melted and smooth. Set aside to cool slightly. Whip the cream with an electric mixer at high speed until stiff peaks form. Transfer the chocolate to another bowl and whisk in ½ cup of the whipped cream. Carefully fold in the remainder of the whipped cream to make a smooth, chocolate whipped cream. Refrigerate until ready to use.

To assemble, spoon the chocolate cream into a pastry bag fitted with a large star tip and pipe it in mounded swirls onto the cooled macaroons. Set the cookies on a baking sheet and freeze until the cream is quite firm (but not frozen), about 20 minutes.

Meanwhile, melt the chocolate for the glaze in the top of a double boiler or in a heatproof bowl set over a pan of simmering (not boiling) water, stirring until smooth. Transfer the chocolate to a medium, deep bowl and let cool to about 90°F (a little below body temperature). Take one cookie at a time from the tray in the freezer and dip it upside down in the chocolate to coat most of the chocolate cream. Let it drip a moment to draw off excess chocolate and set right side up on another baking sheet lined with waxed paper. Gently press an almond on top of the chocolate and repeat with the remaining macaroons. Refrigerate the cookies until the chocolate has set.

Makes 12 servings

Chocolate-Covered Cherry Martini

BALDWIN SALOON, THE DALLES, OREGON

T his goes down very smoothly, just like one of those chocolate-covered cherries surrounded in syrup that you pop in your mouth to eat in one bite. You may need to make a special request at your liquor shop for Cherry Heering liqueur, a not-too-sweet spirit imported from Denmark. It will make a nice addition to your bar for desserts and dessert drinks.

1½ fluid ounces (3 tablespoons) Stolichnaya vanilla vodka

1½ fluid ounces (3 tablespoons) white crème de cacao

¾ fluid ounce (1½ tablespoons) Cherry Heering liqueur

1 teaspoon maraschino cherry juice

½ teaspoon amaretto

Chocolate syrup, for swirling

1 maraschino cherry

Fill a large martini glass with ice and set aside to chill.

Half-fill a cocktail shaker with ice and add the vodka, crème de cacao, cherry liqueur, cherry juice, and amaretto. Cover and shake vigorously until well chilled. Empty the ice from the martini glass, wipe it dry, and line it with chocolate syrup, swirling it around the glass and discarding the excess. Strain the martini mixture into the glass, garnish with the cherry, and serve.

MAKES 1 SERVING

Red, White, and Blue Shortcakes

SOUTH BAY BED AND BREAKFAST, SEDRO-WOOLLEY, WASHINGTON

Definitely not your traditional shortcake, this recipe from innkeeper Sally Moore uses sugar cookies—rather than biscuits—for layering with fruit and whipped cream. The cookies and fillings can be prepared in advance, though the shortcakes should be served right after assembling. The cookies are also quite a tasty snack as is, or spoon some melted chocolate or top-quality jam into the indentation before serving.

½ cup unsalted butter

½ cup granulated sugar, plus more for dipping

1 egg

½ cup vegetable oil

½ cup powdered sugar

½ teaspoon cream of tartar

2½ cups all-purpose flour, more if needed

½ teaspoon baking soda

Strawberries

1½ cups sliced fresh strawberries

1 tablespoon sugar, more to taste

Blueberry Sauce

¾ cup water

½ cup sugar

1 cup fresh blueberries, plus more for serving

1 teaspoon freshly squeezed lemon juice

1 tablespoon cornstarch dissolved in 2 tablespoons cold water

Whipped Cream

1 cup whipping cream

2 tablespoons powdered sugar

½ teaspoon vanilla extract

Mint sprigs, for garnish

Put the strawberries in a small bowl, sprinkle with sugar to taste, and gently toss to mix. Let sit at room temperature to macerate while you bake the cookies (or for 30 to 60 minutes if the cookies are already baked).

For the blueberry sauce, combine the water and sugar in a small saucepan and bring just to a boil over medium-high heat, stirring to help the sugar dissolve. Simmer for 3 minutes. Add ¾ cup of the blueberries and the lemon juice. Reduce the heat to medium and cook, stirring occasionally, until the blueberries soften slightly, about 5 minutes. Stir in the cornstarch mixture and cook, stirring, until thickened and clear, 2 to 3 minutes longer. Stir in the remaining ¼ cup blueberries, take the pan from the heat, and set aside to cool completely.

Preheat the oven to 350°F.

Cream together the butter and granulated sugar in an electric mixer at medium-high speed until light and fluffy, 3 to 4 minutes. Add the egg and beat until incorporated. Add the oil and beat until blended. In a small bowl, stir together the powdered sugar and cream of tartar and add to the butter mixture, blending until smooth and creamy. Sift together the flour and

baking soda and add it a cup at a time, blending well at low speed between additions. The dough should be pliable but not sticky. If necessary, add a bit more flour. Shape the dough into balls of a rounded tablespoon each and set on an ungreased baking sheet about 2 inches apart. Dip the bottom of a lightly damp glass in granulated sugar and press down on each ball of dough until it is about ½ inch thick. Bake until the cookies have risen and are firm to the touch but not browned, about 12 minutes. As soon as they come out of the oven, press each cookie with the same sugared glass to make an indentation in the middle of each cookie. Allow to cool on the baking sheet for a few minutes, then transfer to a wire rack to cool completely.

For the whipped cream, whip the cream in an electric mixer until soft peaks form, add the powdered sugar and vanilla, and continue whipping to stiff peaks.

To serve, put 1 or 2 cookies on each plate. Spoon a scant tablespoon of blueberry sauce into the indentation on each cookie (try to avoid overflow). Arrange sliced strawberries to cover the blueberries, top with a small dollop of the cream and another cookie. Top with more cream, a slice of strawberry, and a couple of whole blueberries. Garnish the plate with more berries and a sprig of fresh mint. Serve right away.

Makes 6 to 12 servings

Mrs. King's Cookies

Highland Inn, Friday Harbor, Washington

A s is true of many homemade cookies, these are best eaten still a bit warm from the oven, with a fresh steaming cup of coffee alongside or maybe a chilled glass of milk to relive a taste of childhood. Innkeeper Helen Chapman King has rightfully gained renown for this cookie recipe, which while familiar in the chocolate chip cookie vein offers some delicious surprises with the array of ingredients used. There is just enough dough to hold them all together!

1 cup unsalted butter

1 cup packed dark brown sugar

1 cup granulated sugar

2 eggs

2 tablespoons freshly squeezed orange juice

1 tablespoon grated orange zest

1 teaspoon vanilla extract

2 cups all-purpose flour

1 teaspoon baking powder

1 teaspoon baking soda

½ teaspoon salt

1½ cups raisins

1½ cups chopped toasted walnuts or pecans

1½ cups good granola, preferably unsweetened

1 cup white chocolate chips

1 cup semisweet chocolate chips

1 cup rolled oats

Preheat the oven to 350°F.

Cream together the butter, brown sugar, and granulated sugar with an electric mixer at medium speed until light and fluffy. Beat in the eggs, orange juice, orange zest, and vanilla until smooth, scraping down the sides of the bowl as needed.

Sift together the flour, baking powder, baking soda, and salt into a medium bowl. Stir the dry ingredients into the batter just until evenly blended. Stir in the raisins, nuts, granola, white and semisweet chocolate chips, and oats.

Form the dough into golf-ball sized balls of about 2 level tablespoons each and arrange them on an ungreased baking sheet about 2 inches apart. Bake until firm on top and just beginning to turn brown around the edges, about 15 minutes. Let the cookies sit on the baking sheet for 3 to 5 minutes to firm up a bit. Transfer to a wire rack to cool slightly while baking the remaining cookies.

MAKES 4 DOZEN COOKIES

Double Chocolate Chip Cookies

Stratford Manor Bed & Breakfast, Bellingham, Washington

ouble the chocolate, double the fun! Both white and semisweet chocolate chips embellish this quick and easy cookie recipe, along with the added flavor from pecan pieces. The cookies make for an addicting afternoon snack.

1¼ cups packed light brown sugar

¾ cup butter-flavored or regular vegetable shortening

2 tablespoons milk

1 tablespoon vanilla extract

1 egg

1¾ cups all-purpose flour

1 teaspoon salt

¾ teaspoon baking soda

1 cup semisweet chocolate chips

¾ cup pecan pieces

½ cup white chocolate chips

Preheat the oven to 375°F.

Cream together the brown sugar, shortening, milk, and vanilla with an electric mixer at medium speed until light and fluffy. Add the egg and mix well.

Stir together the flour, salt, and baking soda in a small bowl. Add the dry ingredients to the creamed mixture and stir to evenly blend. Stir in the semisweet chocolate chips, pecans, and white chocolate chips. Drop by rounded

teaspoonfuls 3 inches apart onto an ungreased baking sheet. Bake until firm to the touch, 8 to 10 minutes. The cookies will appear moist; be careful not to overbake them. Transfer to a wire rack to cool while baking the remaining cookies.

MAKES 3 DOZEN COOKIES

Chocolate Hazelnut Fudge Squares

Canyon Way Restaurant and Bookstore, Newport, Oregon

While not exactly fudge, there is a fudgy-moist quality to the chocolate cake in which a rich chocolate mousse is sandwiched, all drizzled with an equally rich ganache. This is a chocolate-lover's delight, to be sure! All three elements can be made a day ahead, the ganache gently warmed to soften it just before serving. Note that the mousse has uncooked egg in it, should you have concerns about eating raw eggs.

1 cup sugar

1 cup all-purpose flour

½ cup unsweetened cocoa powder

1 teaspoon baking soda

½ teaspoon baking powder

½ teaspoon salt

½ cup sour cream

½ cup espresso or strong coffee

½ cup vegetable oil

1 egg, lightly beaten

1 teaspoon vanilla extract

¾ cup whipping cream

½ cup toasted chopped hazelnuts

Chocolate Mousse

4 ounces top-quality semisweet chocolate, chopped

6 tablespoons unsalted butter

1 tablespoon rum

1 tablespoon coffee or hazelnut liqueur

2 eggs, separated

2 tablespoons sugar

½ teaspoon cream of tartar

¾ cup whipping cream

Ganache

5 ounces top-quality semisweet chocolate, chopped

⅓ cup sugar

¼ cup whipping cream

¼ cup half-and-half

Preheat the oven to 350°F. Lightly butter a 9- by 13-inch baking dish and line the bottom with parchment paper.

Combine the sugar, flour, cocoa powder, baking soda, baking powder, and salt in an electric mixer and mix at low speed just to blend. Add the sour cream, espresso, oil, egg, and vanilla and mix until smooth. Pour the batter into the prepared baking dish and bake until the cake springs back when lightly touched but is still moist (it may seem slightly undercooked), 15 to 18 minutes. Let cool on a wire rack.

For the mousse, melt the chocolate and butter together in the top of a double boiler or in a heatproof bowl set over a pan of simmering (not boiling) water, stirring until smooth. Set aside to cool to room temperature. Slowly whisk the rum and liqueur into the chocolate. Whisk in the egg yolks until smooth and well blended. Whip the egg whites in an electric mixer until

very soft peaks form. Add the sugar and cream of tartar and continue whip-ping until stiff but not dry. In another bowl, whip the cream until soft peaks form. Fold the egg whites into the chocolate mixture, then gently fold in the whipped cream. Refrigerate until ready to use.

For the ganache, combine the chocolate, sugar, cream, and half-and-half in a double boiler or in a heatproof bowl set over a pan of simmering (not boil-ing) water, stirring until the chocolate is melted and the ganache is smooth. Set aside to cool to room temperature.

To assemble, cut the cake into squares, then cut each piece in half horizon-tally. Whip the cream to stiff peaks. Put the bottom half of each cake square on a dessert plate and top with a heaping spoonful of mousse, spreading it out evenly. Add a large spoonful of the whipped cream. Put the other piece of cake on top, press down gently, and drizzle the ganache over the sandwich. Sprinkle with the chopped hazelnuts and serve.

Makes 12 servings

Pies & Tarts

Deep Dish Apple Pie

BALDWIN SALOON, THE DALLES, OREGON

A *nd they do mean deep! This pie is made in a springform pan, where a few vertical inches worth of juicy sweet apples baked with cinnamon and sugar. It makes for quite a treat to serve to your serious dessert-loving friends. Consider an à la mode option, with a scoop of vanilla ice cream served alongside.*

5 to 6 pounds apples, preferably Roma or Gala,
peeled, cored, and cut into eighths

1 cup sugar

¼ cup all-purpose flour

¼ cup water

1 tablespoon ground cinnamon

1 tablespoon freshly squeezed lemon juice

Pie Dough

1½ cups all-purpose flour

½ cup unsalted butter, cut into small pieces and chilled

1 egg yolk

⅓ cup ice water

Topping

1 cup packed light brown sugar

½ cup all-purpose flour

½ cup unsalted butter, cut into small pieces

For the dough, pulse together the flour and butter in a food processor until the mixture has the texture of coarse meal. Add the egg yolk and pulse, then drizzle in the water, pulsing, just until the dough forms a ball (if the dough doesn't form a ball in the machine, turn it out onto the work surface to do so; avoid overworking the dough or it will become tough). Form the dough into a flat disk, wrap it in plastic, and refrigerate for at least 1 hour before rolling it out.

For the topping, combine the brown sugar, flour, and butter in a medium bowl and use your fingers to rub the ingredients together until the butter is the size of small peas. Chill until ready to use.

Preheat the oven to 325°F.

Roll the chilled dough out on a lightly floured work surface to a circle about 18 inches across. Press it into the bottom and up the sides of a 10-inch springform pan. Turn any overhang under at the top of the rim, and crimp decoratively. Refrigerate until ready to fill.

Toss together the apples, sugar, flour, water, cinnamon, and lemon juice in a large bowl until evenly blended. Pour the apple mixture into the prepared pie shell and pack the apples in as tightly as you can, mounding the top slightly.

Sprinkle the topping evenly over the apples and set the pan on a rimmed baking sheet. Bake the pie until the apples are tender when pierced with a knife and the edges are bubbly, about 2 hours. Let cool to room temperature. Refrigerate until ready to serve.

To serve, remove the edges of the springform pan and use a large serrated knife to cut the pie into wedges. Serve at room temperature or warm.

Makes 12 to 16 servings

Fresh Blueberry Tart
with Lavender Crème Fraîche

Pastry chef Stephen Whippo notes that while whole blueberries could be baked directly in the custard tart, he prefers to scatter the berries over the top of the lightly lavender-infused custard so the contrast between the juicy berries and creamy base is more pronounced. He serves the tart slices with a garnish of tangy-sweet candied lemon sections. Note that you need to start at least a day in advance to prepare the crème fraîche for the custard.

The rich, nut-enhanced tart dough is quite tender, so be sure not to skimp too much on the flour when rolling it out. And don't be too distressed if the dough cracks as you work with it; it is soft enough to simply pinch back together.

1 pint fresh blueberries

Lavender Crème Fraîche Custard

2 cups whipping cream

2 teaspoons dried lavender

¼ cup buttermilk

4 eggs

½ cup sugar

½ teaspoon vanilla extract

Almond Cookie Crust

½ cup toasted blanched almonds

3 tablespoons sugar

¾ cup unsalted butter, cut into small pieces and frozen

¾ cup all-purpose flour

½ teaspoon grated lemon zest

⅛ teaspoon salt

1 egg yolk

1 tablespoon whipping cream, more if needed

Lavender Honey Syrup

½ cup sugar

½ cup honey

⅓ cup water

¼ cup fresh blueberries

2 teaspoons dried lavender

For the lavender crème fraîche custard, first make the crème fraîche. Combine the cream and lavender in a small saucepan and bring just to a low simmer over medium heat. Take the pan from the heat and set aside to steep until the cream is at room temperature, about 1 hour. Strain the cream through a fine sieve into a bowl, discarding the lavender. Stir in the buttermilk, cover the bowl with plastic wrap, and set aside in a warm place until quite thick, at least 24 hours. Once thickened, refrigerate until ready to use.

For the crust, pulse the almonds and sugar in a food processor until the almonds are very finely ground. Add the butter and pulse until it is cut into small flakes and the almonds and sugar are sticking to the butter pieces. Add the flour, lemon zest, and salt. Pulse just to blend but stop before the mixture clumps. In a small bowl, whisk together the egg yolk and cream. Pour the mixture into the processor and pulse about a dozen times until the dough is

well blended but has not yet become a solid mass. It should be quite crumbly; pinch a bit between your fingers to confirm that there is enough liquid, and if not drizzle in a bit more cream and pulse a few times to blend. Form the dough into a flat disk, wrap it in plastic, and refrigerate for 1 hour before rolling it out.

For the lavender honey syrup, stir together the sugar, honey, water, ¼ cup blueberries, and lavender in a small saucepan over medium heat and bring to a boil. Remove the pan from the heat, press the berries against the side of the pan to burst, and let steep for 15 minutes. Strain, pressing gently on the berries and lavender to extract their flavor, and discard the solids; set aside to cool. When cool, the consistency should be like honey.

Preheat the oven to 375°F. Lightly oil a 12-inch tart pan with a removable base.

Roll out the chilled dough on a lightly floured work surface to ⅛ inch thick. Gently transfer the dough to the prepared tart pan, pressing it down well into the corners of the pan and laying the excess evenly over the edge of the pan. Roll the rolling pin over the top of the pan to cut away the excess dough, then crimp the edges of the pastry shell to make a neat finish. Prick the bottom of the pastry with the tines of a fork, line with a piece of foil, and add pie weights or dry beans to generously cover the base. Bake the pastry until the edges are lightly browned, about 15 minutes, then carefully remove the foil and weights and continue baking the crust until the base is lightly browned, 5 to 10 minutes longer.

To finish the crème fraîche custard, whisk together the eggs in a medium bowl to blend, then whisk in the lavender crème fraîche, sugar, and vanilla until well blended and the sugar has dissolved. Take the tart shell from the oven and reduce the oven temperature to 275°F. Pour the custard into the

shell and bake until the custard is set, about 50 minutes. Take the tart from the oven and let cool on a wire rack.

Drizzle about half of the syrup over the cooled tart. Top with enough blueberries to evenly cover the surface of the tart. Cut the remaining berries in half, and arrange them randomly cut side up to add color contrast. Refrigerate until ready to serve.

To serve, remove the sides from the tart pan and cut the tart into wedges. Drizzle a dab of the syrup in the center of each plate and top with a slice of tart, then drizzle more of the syrup around the plate.

MAKES 8 SERVINGS

For the dough, toss together the flour, butter, shortening, sugar, and salt in a medium bowl and place in the freezer for 20 minutes. Pour the mixture into a food processor and pulse until the butter pieces are about the size of small peas. Be careful not to overprocess. Pour the mixture back into the medium bowl and add the water, a tablespoon at a time, using your fingertips or a wooden spoon to toss the mixture into a dough. Continue adding water until the dough holds together when pinched. Form the dough into a flat disk, wrap it in plastic, and chill for at least 30 minutes before rolling it out.

Preheat the oven to 375°F.

Roll out the chilled dough on a lightly floured work surface and use it to line a 10-inch deep-dish pie pan. Pierce the bottom all over with the tines of a fork and refrigerate for 30 minutes. Line the chilled crust with foil, fill it with pie weights or dry beans, and bake until the edges are pale golden, about 20 to 25 minutes. Remove the foil and weights and continue baking until the bottom is golden, about 5 to 10 minutes longer. Let the crust cool completely on a wire rack.

For the filling, whisk together the milk and cornstarch in a medium saucepan. Add the sugar, egg yolks, and seeds from the vanilla bean, and whisk well to blend. Cook over medium heat, whisking constantly (it's important to draw the whisk fully across the bottom and sides of the pan to avoid sticking and burning) until bubbling and thick, 4 to 5 minutes. Immediately scrape the custard into a medium bowl to avoid overcooking. Lay a piece of plastic wrap directly on the surface of the custard and let cool to room temperature. When the custard is cooled, whip the cream to soft peaks and fold it into the custard.

Melt the gianduja in the top of a double boiler or in a heatproof bowl set over a pan of simmering (not boiling) water, stirring until smooth. Paint the gianduja over the bottom of the cooled crust. Cut the bananas into ¼-inch slices and arrange them over the chocolate. Spoon the custard filling over and refrigerate until set, at least 1 hour.

Cut the pie into wedges and arrange on individual plates. Top each with a dollop of whipped cream and a sprinkling of toasted chopped hazelnuts.

MAKES 8 SERVINGS

Individual Rustic Blackberry Tarts

YARROW BAY GRILL, KIRKLAND, WASHINGTON

hese generous single-serving tarts from pastry chef Jessica Campbell are easy to make—no tartlet pans needed! The dough rounds are topped with berry filling and the edges of dough folded up over the fruit for a free-form style of tart that's irresistible for no-fuss baking. A drizzle of Whidbey's liqueur, made from loganberries, is an optional addition to the filling but other liqueur can be used in its place.

3 cups fresh blackberries (about ¾ pound)

½ cup plus 2 teaspoons sugar

¼ cup all-purpose flour

2 tablespoons unsalted butter, melted

Grated zest and juice of ½ lemon or orange

2 tablespoons Whidbey's liqueur or Grand Marnier (optional)

Pinch salt

2 tablespoons whipping cream

Vanilla ice cream, for serving

Tart Dough

2 cups all-purpose flour

1 tablespoon sugar

¼ teaspoon salt

¼ teaspoon freshly grated or ground nutmeg

¾ cup unsalted butter, cut into small pieces and chilled

1 egg

1 tablespoon whipping cream

For the dough, combine the flour, sugar, salt, and nutmeg in an electric mixer fitted with the paddle attachment. Mix at medium speed just to blend. Add the butter and beat until the butter is the size of small peas. In a small bowl, whisk together the egg and cream and add this to the flour mixture. Mix just until the dough starts to come together. Form the dough into a flat disk, wrap it in plastic, and refrigerate for at least 1 hour before rolling it out.

Preheat the oven to 375°F. Line 1 large or 2 small baking sheets with parchment paper or a silicone baking mat.

Divide the dough into 4 even pieces. Roll each portion out on a lightly floured work surface to a circle about 9 inches across and ⅛ inch thick.

Toss together the berries, ½ cup of the sugar, the flour, butter, orange or lemon zest and juice, liqueur (if using), and salt in a large bowl. (It's best to do this just before you're ready to assemble the tarts, otherwise the berries give off too much juice.)

Spoon one quarter of the berry filling in the center of one of the pastry circles. Fold the dough edge up around the filling, pleating gently as you go; you should still see the center of the filling. Carefully transfer the tart to a baking sheet and continue with the remaining dough and filling. Brush the tarts with the cream and then sprinkle with the remaining 2 teaspoons sugar. Bake the tarts until they are nicely browned and the filling is bubbling, 30 to 35 minutes. (If baking on 2 racks, shift the pan halfway through cooking.) Serve warm, with vanilla ice cream.

MAKES 4 SERVINGS

Fresh Goat Cheese Tartlets

CAFE BRIO, VICTORIA, BRITISH COLUMBIA

These are surprising tarts. A quick glance at the ingredient list might not do justice to the wonderful flavor that comes from the combination of fresh goat cheese, vanilla bean, and lemon. You can make one large tart—using a 10-inch removable-base pan—rather than individual tartlets, if you prefer.

14 ounces fresh goat cheese

1 cup vanilla sugar (see page 134) or regular granulated sugar

2 vanilla beans, split lengthwise and seeds scraped out

3 eggs

2 teaspoons freshly squeezed lemon juice

Pastry Dough

1½ cups all-purpose flour

3 tablespoons sugar

½ teaspoon salt

½ cup unsalted butter, cut into small pieces and chilled

3 to 4 tablespoons ice water, more if needed

For the pastry dough, combine the flour, sugar, and salt in a food processor and pulse once to mix. Add the butter pieces and pulse to finely chop the butter until it has a coarse, sandy texture. Drizzle the water into the dough 1 tablespoon at a time, again pulsing a few times to just blend in the water. It's important not to overmix the dough or it will be tough rather than flaky. The dough will not form a ball in the machine, but it has the proper amount

of liquid if squeezing some of the dough between your fingers feels neither dusty dry or sticky. Turn the dough out onto the work surface, form it into a flat disk, and wrap it in plastic. Refrigerate the dough for at least 1 hour before rolling it out.

Preheat the oven to 350°F.

Roll out the chilled dough on a lightly floured work surface to about ⅛ inch thick, cut the dough into eight 4½-inch circles, and use them to line 3-inch tartlet pans. Press the dough gently down the sides of each pan to be sure it is evenly covering the bottom. Trim the outer edges of the dough and lightly crimp the edges. Line each tartlet with foil and fill with pie weights or beans. Set the tartlet shells on a baking sheet for easy handling and bake until the edges are set, about 15 minutes. Remove the foil and weights and bake until the bottoms of the tartlets are set and beginning to color, about 10 minutes longer. Set the tartlet shells on a wire rack to cool.

Cream together the goat cheese, vanilla sugar, and vanilla seeds in an electric mixer at medium speed. Add the eggs, one at a time, mixing well after each addition, scraping down the sides of the bowl as needed. Add the lemon juice and mix until smooth. Spoon the filling into the tartlet shells and bake until the filling is set and puffed around the edges, 20 to 25 minutes. Let cool before serving.

MAKES 8 SERVINGS

Vanilla Sugar

To make the vanilla sugar called for in the goat cheese tartlets, you'll have to plan about a week in advance. Bury 2 vanilla beans, folded in half, in about 2 cups of sugar in a small airtight container. Set aside in a cool, dark place for at least a week before using. The vanilla beans will infuse aroma and flavor to the sugar, then the beans can be used for the recipe. After scraping the seeds from the vanilla beans, you can return the vanilla pods to the remaining sugar and continue infusing for another use, adding more sugar as needed to keep the beans covered. Vanilla sugar adds extra flavor to any number of dessert recipes, such as ice cream or crème brûlée. You can use plain granulated sugar instead, however.

Chocolate Nut Pie

FIRST STREET HAVEN, PORT ANGELES, WASHINGTON

*T*his pie is reminiscent of a pecan pie, with a chocolate twist. It is very quick and easy to make, a decadent way to finish a casual dinner with friends. To make this recipe even quicker, buy a frozen pie shell rather than making the dough from scratch.

1 cup semisweet chocolate chips

1 cup walnut pieces

1 cup pecan pieces

1 cup sliced almonds

4 eggs

1 cup light corn syrup

1 cup sugar

½ cup unsalted butter, melted

Lightly sweetened whipped cream, for serving (optional)

Pastry Dough

1½ cups all-purpose flour

3 tablespoons sugar

½ teaspoon salt

½ cup unsalted butter, cut into small pieces and chilled

3 to 4 tablespoons ice water, more if needed

For the pastry dough, combine the flour, sugar, and salt in a food processor and pulse once to mix. Add the butter pieces and pulse to finely chop the butter until it has a coarse, sandy texture. Drizzle the water into the dough

1 tablespoon at a time, again pulsing a few times to just blend in the water. It's important not to overmix the dough or it will be tough rather than flaky. The dough will not form a ball in the machine, but it has the proper amount of liquid if squeezing some of the dough between your fingers feels neither dusty dry or sticky. Turn the dough out onto the work surface, form it into a flat disk, and wrap it in plastic. Refrigerate the dough for at least 30 minutes before rolling it out.

Preheat the oven to 350°F.

Roll out the chilled dough on a lightly floured surface to a roughly 12-inch circle and use it to line a 9- to 10-inch deep-dish pie pan. Press the dough gently down the sides of the pan to be sure it is evenly covering the bottom. Using kitchen shears, trim the outer edge of the dough to a ½-inch overhang, then fold that edge under and use your fingers to crimp the pastry edge.

Scatter the chocolate chips over the bottom of the pie shell, then top with the walnuts, pecans, and almonds. Whisk the eggs in a large bowl just to blend, then whisk in the corn syrup, sugar, and butter until blended. Pour the mixture evenly over the nuts and chips in the pie shell. Bake until the pastry is browned and the filling is set, about 1 hour. (Cover loosely with foil if the top of the pie is well browned before the filling is set.) Let the pie fully cool on a wire rack before cutting into pieces to serve, with a dollop of whipped cream on top if you like.

MAKES 8 TO 12 SERVINGS

Quince Tarte Tatins

CAFE BRIO, VICTORIA, BRITISH COLUMBIA

uince is an old-world tree fruit that looks something like a cross between an apple and a pear, though the firm, tart fruit is inedible raw. Not widely available, quinces appear primarily in the fall in select markets. Apples can be used instead, though you can skip the poaching step and bake the apple half raw. At Cafe Brio, pastry chef Kalyn Sarkany serves these tasty individual tarte Tatins with a caramel sauce embellished with a drizzle of Grand Marnier.

4¼ cups water

4 cups sugar

2 quince (about 8 ounces each), peeled, halved, and cored

1 sheet puff pastry

Topping

¼ cup crème fraîche

¼ cup whipping cream

2 teaspoons powdered sugar

½ teaspoon vanilla extract

Combine 4 cups of the water with 3½ cups of the sugar in a medium saucepan and bring to a boil over medium-high heat, stirring occasionally to help the sugar dissolve. Add the quince, reduce the heat to medium-low, and gently poach the quince until tender when pierced with the tip of a knife, about 40 minutes. Lift the quince from the syrup with a slotted spoon and let cool on a plate in the refrigerator.

For the topping, whisk together the crème fraîche, whipping cream, powdered sugar, and vanilla until stiff peaks form. Refrigerate until ready to serve.

Preheat the oven to 325°F.

Put the remaining ½ cup sugar in a small saucepan with the remaining ¼ cup water. Simmer over medium heat until the sugar has dissolved, stirring occasionally. Continue cooking without stirring until the sugar turns a deep golden color. Remove the sugar from the heat and carefully pour the caramelized sugar into the bottom of four ½-cup ramekins. It will cool and harden almost immediately. (Beware: The ramekins will quickly become quite hot.)

Cut the puff pastry into 4 circles just slightly larger than the size of the ramekin (it will shrink as it cooks) and prick each piece all over with the tines of a fork. Put a quince half, rounded side down, in each ramekin, and set a circle of puff pastry on top. Set the ramekins on a baking sheet for easy handling and bake until the pastry is well browned, about 45 minutes. Let cool slightly on a wire rack. While the tarts are still warm, set a small plate upside down on top of each one of the ramekins and quickly invert them together, slowly lifting off the ramekin to allow caramel to drip down over the quince. Serve warm with a dollop of the topping.

MAKES 4 SERVINGS

Lemon Tart

AQUA RIVA, VANCOUVER, BRITISH COLUMBIA

*A*t Aqua Riva, this recipe is made in individual tartlets, which you can do as well, using six tartlet pans about 4½ inches across. Cooking the lemon tart covered keeps the surface from coloring at all, so it maintains a very soft, creamy yellow color.

1¼ cups sugar

⅔ cup freshly squeezed lemon juice (about 3 large lemons)

⅔ cup whipping cream

3 whole eggs, lightly beaten

2 egg yolks, lightly beaten

Tart Dough

5 tablespoons unsalted butter, at room temperature

¼ cup sugar

1 whole egg

1 egg yolk

1½ cups all-purpose flour

For the tart dough, cream together the butter and sugar with an electric mixer at medium speed until light and fluffy. Lightly beat together the whole egg and egg yolk in a small bowl, add them to the mixer, and mix well. Add the flour all at once and mix together by hand until well combined. Form the dough into a flat disk, wrap it in plastic, and refrigerate for at least 1 hour before rolling it out.

Roll out the chilled dough on a lightly floured work surface to about ⅛ inch thick. Line a 10-inch removable-base tart pan with the dough, pressing it well down into the corners and trimming the top even with the pan edge, pressing the edge gently into the fluted sides. Use a fork to prick the bottom all over and put the tart shell in the freezer for 15 minutes.

Preheat the oven to 350°F.

When the shell is frozen, bake it until set and lightly browned, about 25 minutes. Set aside to cool on a wire rack and reduce the oven temperature to 325°F.

Whisk together the sugar, lemon juice, and cream in a large bowl. Add the whole eggs and egg yolks and whisk well. Press the mixture through a strainer into a lipped bowl or measuring cup, then pour it into the cooled tart shell.

Put the tart on a baking sheet and lay another baking sheet on top of the tart, or cover it loosely with a piece of foil so that it doesn't touch the filling. Bake the tart for 45 minutes. The filling will look as if it is not set when you take the tart from the oven; it should jiggle a little in the center. Let the tart cool on a wire rack to room temperature. Refrigerate until set and fully chilled before serving.

MAKES 8 SERVINGS

Cherry and Ricotta Tartlets

WILDWOOD RESTAURANT, PORTLAND, OREGON

The Portland Farmers Market is such an inspiration for writing the Wildwood dessert menu," notes the restaurant's pastry chef, Gretchen Glatte. This recipe is among those she has demonstrated at the market. "The kirsch I use in this recipe is amazing and produced at Clear Creek Distillery, just around the corner from our restaurant. I believe it makes the dessert exquisite." This recipe can also be used to make one large 10-inch tart.

2 cups pitted, halved dark sweet cherries (about ½ pound)

¼ cup Clear Creek Distillery kirsch or other brandy

1½ cups ricotta cheese

1 to 2 tablespoons honey or sugar, or to taste

½ vanilla bean, split lengthwise and seeds scraped out, or
1 teaspoon vanilla extract

2 tablespoons whipping cream

¼ cup sliced almonds, toasted

½ cup shaved or grated top-quality bittersweet chocolate

Honey Butter Tart Dough

1 cup unsalted butter, at room temperature

¼ cup sugar

¼ cup honey

2½ cups all-purpose flour

1 teaspoon salt

½ teaspoon ground cinnamon, finely ground black pepper,
or ground anise (optional)

Combine the cherries and kirsch in a medium bowl, tossing gently to mix. Cover with plastic and let sit while making the tart dough. (The cherries will have better flavor if you do this the night before making the tart, in which case the mixture should be refrigerated.)

For the tart dough, cream together the butter, sugar, and honey in an electric mixer at medium speed until light and fluffy. Add the flour, salt, and spice (if using) and mix at low speed until the dough comes together, scraping the sides of the bowl as needed. Form the dough into a flat disk, wrap it in plastic, and refrigerate for at least 1 hour before rolling it out.

Preheat the oven to 350°F.

Roll out the chilled dough on a lightly floured work surface to about ⅛ inch thick. Cut the dough into 5-inch circles and use them to line eight 4-inch tartlet pans, trimming off any excess. Freeze the tarts for about 30 minutes.

Set the tartlet pans on a baking sheet for easy handling and prick the bottoms with the tines of a fork. Bake the tartlet shells until deep golden brown, 15 to 20 minutes. Set aside on a wire rack to cool.

Stir together the ricotta, honey to taste, and the vanilla bean seeds or extract until well blended. Add the cream and stir until smooth. Spoon the ricotta into the cooled tartlet shells. Drain the cherries and arrange them cut side down on the filling. Sprinkle with the almonds and chocolate and serve right away.

MAKES 8 SERVINGS

Rustic Pear Tart with Hazelnuts

HUDSON'S BAR AND GRILL, VANCOUVER, WASHINGTON

*P*ears and hazelnuts are an ideal match, both echoing flavors of fall in the Northwest. Ripe, juicy pears will provide the best flavor for this tart, but if the pears you're using are quite ripe, take care not to overcook them so that they hold their shape, rather than becoming a purée.

3 tablespoons unsalted butter

3 medium ripe pears (about 1½ pounds), skins left on, cored, and diced

¼ cup plus 2 tablespoons packed brown sugar

¼ cup all-purpose flour

¼ teaspoon ground cinnamon

¼ teaspoon salt

1 egg

1 tablespoon cold water

¼ cup chopped toasted hazelnuts

Tart Dough

1½ cups all-purpose flour

2 tablespoons granulated sugar

½ teaspoon salt

5 tablespoons unsalted butter, cut into pieces and chilled

¼ cup cold water

2 egg yolks

Preheat the oven to 375°F. Line a large baking sheet with parchment paper or a silicone baking mat.

For the tart dough, stir together the flour, sugar, and salt in a large bowl. Cut in the butter until crumbly. (Alternatively, pulse together the flour, sugar, and salt in a food processor, add the butter pieces, and pulse until the mixture has the texture of coarse meal. Transfer to a large bowl.) In a small bowl, whisk together the cold water and egg yolks and add this to the dry mixture, stirring just until the dough comes together. Form the dough into a flat disk, wrap it in plastic, and refrigerate for 30 minutes before rolling it out.

Roll out the dough on a lightly floured surface to a circle about 14 inches across. Transfer the circle to the baking sheet and chill while preparing the filling.

Melt the butter in a large skillet over medium heat. Add the pears, ¼ cup of the brown sugar, the flour, cinnamon, and salt. Sauté the mixture until the brown sugar is melted and the ingredients are well blended, 2 to 3 minutes. Set aside to cool. When the filling has cooled to room temperature, spoon it into the center of the prepared tart dough, leaving a 3-inch border. Fold the dough up around the filling, pleating gently as you go; you should still see the center of the filling. Lightly beat the egg with the cold water and brush the tart with the mixture. Sprinkle the remaining 2 tablespoons brown sugar and the hazelnuts over the tart. Bake until the pears are tender and the crust is golden brown, about 30 minutes. Let cool on a wire rack before cutting into wedges to serve.

MAKES 6 TO 8 SERVINGS

Frozen Desserts

White Chocolate Grapefruit Ice Cream

DUCK SOUP INN, FRIDAY HARBOR, WASHINGTON

A surprising combination, this recipe ends a meal with a rich but brightly flavored indulgence. The white chocolate contributes richness and sweetness, while the grapefruit zest contrasts with vibrant citrus flavors.

1 small pink grapefruit

⅔ cup plus ½ cup sugar

¼ cup water

7 egg yolks

3 cups half-and-half

5 ounces top-quality white chocolate, chopped

1 cup whipping cream

Fresh mint, julienned, for serving

Grate enough zest from the grapefruit to make 1 tablespoon and set aside. Cut the sections from the grapefruit (see page 53). Combine ½ cup of the sugar and the water in a small saucepan and bring just to a boil over medium heat, stirring to help the sugar dissolve. Add the grapefruit sections and reduce the heat to low. Cook gently to lightly sweeten the grapefruit, about 10 minutes. Lift the sections out with a fork and drain on paper towels. Set aside for garnishing the ice cream. (The grapefruit sections can be wrapped in plastic and refrigerated until ready to serve, up to a day in advance.)

Whisk together the egg yolks and the remaining ⅔ cup sugar in a medium heatproof bowl until smooth and pale yellow in color. Add the grapefruit zest and whisk to blend. Slowly whisk in 2 cups of the half-and-half until fully

incorporated. Put the bowl over a pan of simmering (not boiling) water, being careful to not let the water touch the bottom of the bowl. Cook, stirring constantly with a rubber spatula and scraping the bottom of the bowl, until the mixture thickens, 5 to 7 minutes. Take the bowl from the heat and stir in the chopped chocolate until melted. Stir in the remaining 1 cup of the half-and-half and the cream. Chill over a bowl of ice water or in the refrigerator until completely cold. Freeze in an ice cream maker according to the manufacturer's instructions, then transfer to an airtight container and freeze until set, at least 2 hours. Scoop the ice cream into individual bowls and surround with the grapefruit sections, scattering the fresh mint on top.

MAKES 1½ QUARTS

Rainier Pavlova with Douglas Fir Sorbet and Macerated Berries

CASCADIA, SEATTLE, WASHINGTON

At Cascadia, this dessert gets a dramatic final flourish: The snow-capped mountain of sorbet-filled meringue is surrounded by a swath of cotton candy, which looks like a layer of low-lying clouds beneath the mountaintop. One of the prides of chef-owner Kerry Sear's kitchen is the big cotton candy machine, authentic Coney Island style, that he brought back from the East Coast. It spins delicate sugar that finishes off many Cascadia desserts.

This sorbet also stars as the centerpiece for Cascadia's signature alpine martini. To make it at home, simply add a small scoop of the sorbet to well-chilled Absolut Citron vodka in a martini glass. Douglas fir abounds in the Northwest (it is, in fact, Oregon's state tree). Call on your foraging skills (or those of a friend) to find some for this recipe, collecting it away from areas where spraying may occur. Be sure to rinse it well before using.

¼ cup water

2 to 3 tablespoons sugar

3 cups mixed fresh berries

2 to 3 tablespoons Grand Marnier or kirsch

Powdered sugar, for serving

Douglas Fir Sorbet

2 cups water

1 cup sugar

10 to 12 1-inch lengths of tender Douglas fir, plus more for garnish

1 tablespoon gin

Meringue

¾ cup sugar

1 tablespoon cornstarch

3 egg whites

¼ teaspoon salt

¼ teaspoon cream of tartar

1½ teaspoons white vinegar

¾ teaspoon vanilla extract

For the Douglas fir sorbet, combine 1 cup of the water with the sugar and Douglas fir in a small saucepan. Bring to a boil over medium-high heat, stirring to help the sugar dissolve, reduce the heat to medium, and simmer for 10 minutes. Strain the syrup into a medium bowl and let cool. Stir in the remaining cup of water and the gin, then refrigerate until fully chilled. Pour the mixture into an ice cream maker and freeze according to the man-ufacturer's instructions. Transfer the sorbet to an airtight container and freeze until set, at least 2 hours.

For the berries, combine the water and sugar in a small saucepan and cook over medium heat, stirring, until the sugar dissolves. Take the pan from the heat and let cool completely. Stir in the berries and the Grand Marnier or kirsch. Set aside until ready to serve.

For the meringue, preheat the oven to 230°F.

Sift together the sugar and cornstarch; set aside. Begin whipping the egg whites, salt, and cream of tartar in an electric mixer at medium speed until frothy, then continue whipping at high speed until very soft peaks form. Gradually add the sugar mixture and, when all the sugar is added, continue

whipping for 5 minutes longer. Reduce the speed to low and drizzle in the vinegar and vanilla. Mix just until evenly blended.

Line a large baking sheet with parchment paper or a silicone baking mat. Using a rubber spatula, scoop the meringue onto the baking sheet, forming 8 oblong mounds that resemble a pillow, about 4 by 2½ inches. Form little spikes of meringue coming out from the 4 corners of the "pillow" by pressing the spatula gently into the corner and slowly drawing the spatula outward. Allow about 2 inches between each of the meringues. Bake until the meringues puff slightly, are firm to the touch, and just very lightly browned, about 1½ hours. They will crisp up more after being removed from the oven; set aside on a wire rack to cool, still on the baking sheet.

To serve, use a small knife to break away the top center of each meringue, exposing the soft center and reserving the broken meringue bits. Set a meringue on each plate and add a scoop of Douglas fir sorbet to the center. Spoon the macerated berries and some of their liquid over and around the sorbet, scattering the meringue bits on top. Add a generous sprinkle of powdered sugar to the pavlova and serve right away, garnished with a sprig of Douglas fir if you like.

Makes 8 servings

Star Anise Ice Cream

R honda Viani creates a number of delicious ice creams at this popular Vancouver restaurant. This aromatic ice cream is infused with the warm flavor of exotic star anise, which is available in well-stocked grocery stores and specialty food shops. Viani serves this atop her Wildflower Honey-Roasted Strawberries (page 64).

I cup whipping cream

I cup milk

4 star anise

¼ vanilla bean, split lengthwise

I cup sugar

6 egg yolks

Combine the cream, milk, star anise, and vanilla bean in a medium saucepan over medium-high heat and bring just to a boil. Set aside; steep for 15 minutes.

In a medium bowl, whisk together the sugar and egg yolks until well blended and the color turns pale yellow. Slowly add the warm cream mixture to the bowl, whisking constantly, then pour this back into the saucepan. Cook the custard over medium-low heat, stirring constantly with a wooden spoon, until the custard thickens enough to coat the back of the spoon, 5 to 7 minutes. Pour the custard into another bowl and let cool (nesting it in a larger bowl of ice water will speed up this process). Refrigerate until fully chilled.

Strain the custard, discarding the star anise and vanilla bean. Pour the mixture into an ice cream maker and freeze according to the manufacturer's instructions. Transfer the ice cream to an airtight container and freeze until set, at least 2 hours.

Makes about 1 quart

Icebox Passion Fruit Soufflé

T his is a popular summertime dessert on the menu at The Teahouse, where the frozen soufflé is formed in individual dessert rings. Childhood favorite Rice Krispies add tasty crunch to the dark chocolate base, also embellished with cashews, a contrast to the creamy-tangy passion fruit mousse. (Note that this recipe calls for uncooked eggs, should you have concerns about eating raw eggs.)

Passion fruit is a tropical fruit that has black seeds covered with a highly aromatic, citrusy pulp. If you can find ripe passion fruit (check high-end grocery stores), scoop the pulpy seeds into a strainer and press the pulp through with the back of a spoon, leaving the seeds behind. Otherwise, look for passion fruit purée in specialty food stores or well-stocked grocery stores.

5 eggs, separated

1¼ cups sugar

⅓ cup passion fruit purée

Pinch salt

1¾ cups whipping cream

Crust

4 ounces top-quality bittersweet chocolate, chopped

¾ cup Rice Krispies™

¾ cup chopped toasted cashews

Line the base of a 10-inch springform pan with a round of parchment paper.

For the crust, melt the chocolate in the top of a double boiler or in a medium heatproof bowl set over a pan of simmering (not boiling) water, stirring occasionally until melted and smooth. Take the bowl from the heat

and stir in the Rice Krispies and cashews until they are evenly coated in chocolate. Add the crust mixture by spoonfuls to the springform pan, pressing down with the back of the spoon to lightly flatten each addition. You don't necessarily need to cover the bottom thoroughly, but spread it out as evenly as possible. Refrigerate the crust while you make the soufflé.

Beat the egg yolks in an electric mixer at medium-high speed until they are pale yellow. Add ¼ cup of the sugar and beat until light and fluffy. Slowly add the passion fruit purée and continue beating until well blended. Set aside.

Beat the egg whites and salt in an electric mixer at high speed until frothy. With the mixer running at medium speed, gradually add the remaining 1 cup sugar. Continue beating until the egg whites are glossy and light but not stiff. Set aside. Whip the cream with an electric mixer at medium-high speed to soft peaks.

Gently fold a bit of the egg whites into the passion fruit mixture to lighten. Fold in the rest of the whites in 2 additions. Fold a bit of this mixture into the whipped cream and then fold the cream into the remaining passion fruit mixture in 3 additions. Scoop the soufflé mixture into the springform pan, smoothing the top evenly. Cover the pan with plastic wrap and freeze until set, at least 3 hours, preferably overnight. Just before serving, run a small thin knife blade around the outside of the frozen soufflé, remove the sides of the pan, and cut the soufflé into wedges to serve.

Makes 12 servings

Parchment Rounds

For an easy way to cut a round of parchment paper to fit in the bottom of a round pan, begin by cutting a square of paper just a bit larger than the pan. Fold the paper in half, then in half again to form quarters, again into eights, and continue folding the paper in half a few more times to form a slender wedge. Turn the pan over and hold the paper flat against the pan so that the tip is in the center of the pan. Use kitchen shears to cut the paper in a slight arc just inside the outer edge of the pan. Unfold the paper and you should have a circle that will fit perfectly inside the baking pan.

Roasted Plum Sorbet

THIRD FLOOR FISH CAFE, KIRKLAND, WASHINGTON

T he inspiration for this recipe," explains pastry chef Sandra Watson, "came one year when my Santa Rosa plum tree had way more plums than my family could ever use." The roasting of the plums develops a wonderful deep flavor, which is complemented by the addition of black pepper. It is one truly distinctive sorbet.

4 pounds Santa Rosa or other red plums, pitted and quartered

2 teaspoons freshly squeezed lemon juice

1¾ cups sugar

¾ teaspoon freshly ground black pepper

1 vanilla bean, split lengthwise and seeds scraped out

¼ teaspoon ground cinnamon

⅓ cup port

Preheat the oven to 350°F.

Toss the plums with the lemon juice in a large bowl. Stir together the sugar, black pepper, vanilla bean seeds, and cinnamon in a small bowl. Scatter this over the plums and toss to evenly coat them. Pour the plums into a large roasting pan and bake until the plums are tender and have a deep, roasty aroma, stirring occasionally, about 1 hour.

Take the pan from the oven and let cool completely on a wire rack. Purée the plums with the accumulated juices in a food processor or blender (working in

batches if needed) until completely smooth. Transfer the purée to a bowl, stir in the port, and refrigerate until fully chilled, at least a few hours or over-night. Pour the mixture into an ice cream maker and freeze according to the manufacturer's instructions. Transfer the sorbet to an airtight container and freeze until set, at least 2 hours.

MAKES ABOUT 1½ QUARTS

Honey Rosemary Ice Cream

HUNT CLUB, SEATTLE, WASHINGTON

*T*his is a simple recipe but one that marries flavor and richness with surprising herbal elements from fresh rosemary. Delicious with a simple drizzle of chocolate sauce or fresh berry coulis, this ice cream would also be an interesting complement to a deep chocolate cake, such as the Double-Baked Chocolate Cake (page 2).

4 cups half-and-half

1 ounce (about four 2-inch sprigs) fresh rosemary

7 egg yolks

¾ cup honey

½ cup sugar

Bring the half-and-half and rosemary to a simmer in a medium saucepan over medium-high heat. Take the pan from the heat, cover with the lid or a piece of foil, and set aside to steep for 30 minutes.

Beat together the egg yolks, honey, and sugar with an electric mixer at medium-high speed until the mixture thickens and turns pale yellow (you can also do this by hand, beating vigorously with a large whisk). Strain the half-and-half into a lipped container, discarding the rosemary. With the mixer at low speed, gradually drizzle in the warm half-and-half. Blend until the mixture is smooth. Pour the custard back into the medium saucepan and cook over medium-low heat, stirring constantly with a wooden spoon until the mixture is thick enough to coat the back of a spoon, 3 to 5 minutes.

Take the pan from the heat and strain immediately into a shallow pan (to help dissipate the heat and cool the mixture more efficiently). Cool as rapidly as possible, either over an ice bath or in the refrigerator. When the mixture is cold, freeze in an ice cream maker according to the manufacturer's instructions. Transfer the ice cream to an airtight container and freeze until set, at least 2 hours.

MAKES ABOUT 1½ QUARTS

Frozen Strawberry and Lemon Terrine

HIGGINS RESTAURANT AND BAR, PORTLAND, OREGON

*T*his is a very pretty dessert with pastel layers of lemon and strawberry, great for a dinner party, especially since the terrine is assembled in advance and frozen until ready to serve. The nutty coating of ground almonds adds a contrast of flavor, color, and texture to the terrine, but you can omit that if you prefer—the terrine is quite delicious on its own.

⅓ cup strawberry preserves

¾ cup whole blanched almonds, toasted (optional)

Sliced strawberries, for garnish

Lemon Mousse

½ cup whipping cream

½ cup freshly squeezed lemon juice

½ cup sugar

4 egg yolks

1 tablespoon finely grated lemon zest

Strawberry Mousse

½ cup whipping cream

⅔ cup puréed strawberries (about 10 ounces whole berries, stemmed)

½ cup sugar

4 egg yolks

Line a 9- by 5-inch loaf pan or other 1½-quart terrine mold with plastic wrap; set aside.

For the lemon mousse, whip the cream with an electric mixer at high speed until soft peaks form. Refrigerate the whipped cream until ready to use. Combine the lemon juice, sugar, egg yolks, and lemon zest in the top of a double boiler or in a medium heatproof bowl and whisk to blend. Set the bowl over a pan of simmering (not boiling) water and whip constantly with a handheld beater at medium speed or a whisk until the mixture is fluffy and thickened, 4 to 5 minutes. Take the mousse from the heat, strain it through a fine sieve, and continue whipping until cool. When the mousse is cooled, fold in the whipped cream. Spoon the mousse into the prepared mold, smooth the surface as much as possible, and freeze while making the strawberry mousse.

For the strawberry mousse, repeat the technique, replacing the lemon juice and zest with the strawberry purée. When the lemon mousse layer is frozen, take the mold from the freezer and spread the strawberry preserves over the lemon mousse. Spoon the strawberry mousse over the preserves and spread the surface evenly. Wrap the mold in plastic and freeze until solid, at least 6 hours or preferably overnight.

For the nut coating (if using), pulse the almonds in a food processor to finely chop them; be careful to avoid overprocessing or the almonds will turn to a paste. Store in an airtight container until ready to use. (The almonds can be chopped up to a day in advance.)

Just before serving, spread the ground almonds in a rectangle just about the size of the long edge of the mold. Dip the bottom of the mold into a bowl of warm, not hot, water for a few seconds (avoid getting water in the terrine). Unmold the terrine, discard the plastic, and press each side of the terrine into the nuts to lightly coat the surface, patting to remove excess. Set the terrine on a platter and serve right away or freeze for an hour or two before slicing. Serve with fresh strawberries alongside.

MAKES 8 TO 10 SERVINGS

The Palace Float with Mascarpone Sherbet

T his float is a great combo of colors and flavors—red, white, and green; bitter, sweet, citrus, and creamy. At Palace they serve the sherbets in a glass bowl and set the little bottle of San Pellegrino Sanbitter—a bright red, bittersweet soda—right alongside for the diner to pour over the top. Look for this bitter in gourmet or import food shops, or use another slightly bitter soda such as San Pellegrino's Aranciata (orange) or Limonata (lemon), which are more commonly available. If you like, you can serve this float in a more traditional way, in a tall glass with a spoon and a straw.

Pastry chefs at Palace make both sherbets for this float, but since most home cooks can make only one flavor at a time, you can simply make the mascarpone sherbet and purchase a good quality lime sherbet or sorbet. (If you choose to make both, try the Lime Sorbet on page 84.) The mascarpone sherbet, rich and almost buttery in texture but lighter than a traditional ice cream, would also be nice scooped on other desserts, such as a fresh blackberry crisp or a plate of figs roasted with honey.

4 scoops top-quality lime sherbet or sorbet

4 small bottles San Pellegrino Sanbitter

Mascarpone Sherbet

¾ cup sugar

¾ cup water

16 ounces mascarpone, at room temperature

2¼ teaspoons freshly squeezed lemon juice

Pinch salt

For the mascarpone sherbet, combine the sugar and water in a small saucepan and bring to a simmer over medium-high heat, stirring occasionally until the sugar is dissolved. Take the pan from the heat and set aside to cool.

When the syrup is at room temperature, combine the mascarpone, syrup, lemon juice, and salt in a medium bowl and gently whisk until smooth (avoid overwhipping or the mixture will become quite stiff). Refrigerate until fully chilled. Freeze in an ice cream maker according to the manufacturer's instructions. Transfer the sherbet to an airtight container and freeze until firm, for several hours or overnight.

To make the float, put a scoop of the mascarpone sherbet and a scoop of lime sherbet in a glass bowl, and serve with the bottle of San Pellegrino Sanbittèr alongside for pouring over the sherbet as you eat.

MAKES 4 SERVINGS

Chocolate Gelato

Turtleback Farm Inn, Orcas Island, Washington

his recipe simply could not be any easier—you don't even have to melt any chocolate, as the rich chocolate flavor comes from cocoa powder. Innkeeper Susan Fletcher likes to run the gelato through the food processor after it has been churned in the ice cream machine and frozen just until firm. This step breaks up the ice crystals even further to produce a lighter gelato, which you can also do if you find the texture of the gelato to be too firm. The food processor comes in handy as well if you don't have an ice cream machine. You can simply freeze the gelato base in a shallow pan, breaking it up with a fork occasionally as it freezes to make it slushy. When solid, break the gelato into pieces for a whirl in the food processor.

While tasty as is with just a cookie alongside or a sprinkling of fresh berries on top, this would also make a delicious accompaniment to the Coconut Cream Cake (page 175). Adding a teaspoon or two of instant espresso powder to the gelato base will give the dessert even deeper flavor.

3 cups milk

¾ cup sugar

¾ cup unsweetened cocoa powder

2 teaspoons cornstarch

Whisk together 1 cup of the milk with the sugar, cocoa powder, and cornstarch; set aside.

Bring the remaining 2 cups of milk to a simmer in a medium saucepan over medium heat. Take the pan from the heat and stir in the cocoa mixture. Return the pan to the heat and cook until the sugar and cocoa dissolve and the mixture just comes to a low boil, 2 to 3 minutes. Transfer to a bowl and set aside to cool at room temperature. Cover with plastic wrap and refrigerate until fully chilled, preferably overnight.

Freeze the gelato in an ice cream maker according to the manufacturer's directions. Transfer the gelato to an airtight freezer container and freeze until set, about 2 hours. The gelato will be easier to serve if it sits out for 15 to 20 minutes before serving.

MAKES ABOUT 1 QUART

The Chocolate Raspberry

GEISER GRAND HOTEL, BAKER CITY, OREGON

onderful aroma and flavor emerge from this decadent after–dinner cocktail, a blend of vanilla, chocolate, and raspberry. Just the thing to sip alongside the Chocolate Raspberry Cake (page 23).

1 fluid ounce (2 tablespoons) Stolichnaya vanilla vodka

1 fluid ounce (2 tablespoons) Godiva liqueur

1 fluid ounce Chambord

1 whole fresh raspberry, for garnish

Fill a large martini glass with ice and set aside to chill.

Half-fill a cocktail shaker with ice and add the vodka, Godiva, and Chambord. Cover the shaker and shake vigorously until well chilled. Discard the ice from the martini glass and strain the cocktail into the chilled martini glass. Add the raspberry to the glass and serve right away.

MAKES 1 SERVING

Raspberry Swirl Ice Cream

WEST, VANCOUVER, BRITISH COLUMBIA

*T*his is the perfect match for the Chocolate Raspberry Cake (page 23) from the same popular Vancouver restaurant. For the raspberry purée, start with about 8 ounces of fresh or thawed whole frozen berries and purée them in a food processor or blender. Press the purée through a fine sieve to remove the many seeds; this should give you just about the ½ cup of strained purée needed.

½ cup raspberry purée

¾ cup sugar

1 cup whipping cream

1 cup milk

6 egg yolks

Bring the raspberry purée and ¼ cup of the sugar to a boil in a small saucepan over medium heat, stirring to help the sugar dissolve. Simmer until reduced by half, about 15 minutes. Let cool to room temperature. Refrigerate until fully chilled.

Bring the cream and milk to a boil in a medium saucepan over medium heat. In a small bowl, whisk together the remaining ½ cup sugar and egg yolks until thick and pale. Slowly drizzle about half of the hot cream into the egg mixture, whisking well. Add the egg mixture to the cream in the saucepan. Cook over medium-low heat, stirring constantly with a wooden spoon, until the mixture thickens and coats the back of the spoon, 3 to 5 minutes. Strain

the custard into a clean bowl and set the bowl in a larger bowl of ice water to cool. When cold, freeze the mixture in an ice cream maker according to the manufacturer's instructions. Transfer the ice cream to an airtight container and gently fold in the raspberry purée so there are streaks throughout the ice cream. Freeze in an airtight container until set, at least 2 hours.

MAKES ABOUT 1 QUART

Special Occasions

White Chocolate and Pumpkin Bombe

KASTEEL FRANSSEN, OAK HARBOR, WASHINGTON

The white outer dome of this showy dessert hides a rich amber pumpkin mousse, revealed only when the bombe is cut into wedges to serve. It makes for a splendid dinner party dessert: The work's all done in advance and the bombe can be unmolded onto a serving plate before dinner and kept frozen until just before serving. The large quantity of gelatin used assures that the bombe will hold up well, even as it begins to thaw after unmolding.

White Chocolate Mousse

8 ounces top-quality white chocolate, chopped

⅓ cup sugar

1 whole egg

1 egg yolk

1½ tablespoons unflavored gelatin powder

1½ cups whipping cream

Pumpkin Mousse

½ cup packed light brown sugar

¼ cup rum

1 tablespoon unflavored gelatin powder

½ cup pumpkin purée

Pinch cinnamon

Pinch freshly grated or ground nutmeg

1 cup whipping cream

Chocolate Base

¾ cup whipping cream

2 tablespoons sugar

2 tablespoons unsalted butter

12 ounces semisweet chocolate chips

2 tablespoons Grand Marnier

For the white chocolate mousse, melt the white chocolate in the top of a double boiler or in a heatproof bowl set over a pan of simmering (not boiling) water, stirring until smooth. Set aside to cool slightly. In a separate bowl, whisk together the sugar, whole egg, egg yolk, and gelatin. Whip the cream to medium peaks in an electric mixer at medium-high speed. Whisk the melted chocolate into the egg mixture, then fold in the whipped cream. Pour the mousse mixture into a 3- or 4-quart bowl. Cover the outside of the bottom of a smaller bowl (about 1½ quarts) with plastic wrap and gently press the bowl into the white chocolate mousse to make a depression that is relatively even; don't press the bowl in too deeply or it will touch the bottom of the larger bowl. There should be about 1 inch between the bottoms of the 2 bowls. Freeze the mousse, with both bowls, until set, about 2 hours. Remove the smaller bowl and the plastic and return the mousse to the freezer.

For the pumpkin mousse, combine the brown sugar, rum, and gelatin in the top of a double boiler or in a heatproof bowl set over a pan of simmering (not boiling) water, and whisk until the gelatin has dissolved. Whisk in the pumpkin purée, cinnamon, and nutmeg until smooth; set aside to cool. Whip the cream to medium peaks and fold it into the pumpkin mixture. Spoon the pumpkin mousse into the depression in the white chocolate

mousse (if there's a bit more mousse than will fit in the depression, simply spread it evenly over the whole surface). Freeze for 1 hour.

For the chocolate base, combine the cream, sugar, and butter in a small saucepan and bring to a boil over medium-high heat, stirring occasionally. Add the chocolate chips and Grand Marnier and whisk until the chocolate has melted. Set aside to cool at room temperature. Spread the chocolate mixture over the top of the mousse in the bowl, cover, and freeze overnight.

To unmold, dip the bowl into hot water for a few seconds and set a serving plate upside down on top of the bowl. Invert both together and lift off the bowl. Cut the bombe into wedges to serve.

MAKES 8 TO 12 SERVINGS

Coconut Cream Cake

CAPRIAL'S BISTRO, PORTLAND, OREGON

his cake from pastry chef Melissa Carey-Ragland is a celebration of coconut, with a coconut-flavored cake batter, coconut pastry cream, and toasted coconut covering the surface of the cake. It is a showstopper recipe that will wow your friends. At Caprial's Bistro, they serve the tall slices of cake on a pool of rich chocolate sauce for a perfect finale.

Coconut Pastry Cream Filling

1 cup unsweetened coconut milk

1 cup half-and-half

1 vanilla bean, split lengthwise

4 egg yolks

½ cup sugar

¼ cup cornstarch

1½ cups sweetened shredded coconut

2 teaspoons vanilla extract

1 cup whipping cream

Cake

2 cups sugar

1 cup unsalted butter, cut into small pieces

4 eggs

2 teaspoons vanilla extract

3 cups sifted cake flour

1 tablespoon baking powder

¾ teaspoon salt

1¼ cups unsweetened coconut milk

1 to 1½ cups sweetened shredded coconut, for garnish

Quick Buttercream

2 cups half-and-half

3 tablespoons cornstarch

1 egg yolk

2 cups unsalted butter, at room temperature

¾ cup sugar

⅛ teaspoon salt

1 tablespoon vanilla extract

For the pastry cream, bring the coconut milk, half-and-half, and vanilla bean to a boil in a heavy saucepan over medium heat. Meanwhile, whisk together the egg yolks, sugar, and cornstarch in a large bowl. Slowly whisk about half of the hot coconut milk mixture into the egg mixture to gently warm it, then whisk in the remaining hot coconut milk mixture. Scrape the seeds from inside the vanilla bean into the custard and discard the bean. Pour the mixture back into the saucepan and cook over medium heat, whisking constantly, until it just comes to a boil and is very thick, 3 to 5 minutes. Transfer the pastry cream to a clean large bowl and whisk in the coconut and vanilla. Lay a piece of plastic wrap on the surface of the pastry cream so that it doesn't form a skin and refrigerate until well chilled, about 2 hours.

Preheat the oven to 350°F. Butter two 9-inch cake pans and line the bottoms with parchment paper.

For the cake, cream together the sugar and butter in an electric mixer fitted with the paddle attachment at medium-high speed, scraping down the sides of the bowl often, until light and fluffy, about 5 minutes. With the mixer at low speed, add the eggs, one at a time, scraping down the sides of the bowl and mixing well after each addition. Add the vanilla and mix well. Combine the flour, baking powder, and salt in another bowl. Add half of the dry ingredients to the batter and beat on low speed until well blended. Beat in half of the coconut milk. Add the remaining dry ingredients followed by the remaining coconut milk, beating well after each addition.

Divide the batter between the cake pans and bake until the cake springs back when touched lightly in the center, 35 to 40 minutes. Let cool for 10 minutes. Remove the cakes from the pans and let cool completely on a wire rack. Leave the oven set at 350°F.

Spread the shredded coconut on a baking sheet. Bake until golden brown and aromatic, 8 to 10 minutes, stirring a few times to ensure the coconut toasts evenly. Let cool completely on the pan.

For the buttercream, combine the half-and-half, cornstarch, and egg yolk in a medium saucepan and whisk until smooth. Cook over medium-high heat, whisking constantly, until it comes to a boil and is very thick. (You should be able to see the bottom of the pan as you stir.) Strain the mixture into a bowl, pressing it through with a rubber spatula, and refrigerate until cool, about 30 minutes. When the mixture has cooled, cream together the butter and sugar at high speed in an electric mixer fitted with the paddle attachment, scraping down the sides of the bowl occasionally, until very light, fluffy, and white, 8 to 10 minutes. Add the salt and mix well. With the mixer on low speed, slowly add the cooled half-and-half mixture, scraping down the sides of the bowl, and mix until smooth. Add the vanilla and mix well.

To finish the filling, whip the cream in an electric mixer at high speed until soft peaks form. Fold the whipped cream into the pastry cream until smooth.

To assemble the cake, use a serrated knife to halve the cake layers horizontally. Set one half, cut side up, on the serving plate and spread one-third of the coconut pastry cream filling over the cake. Top with another cake layer and repeat the layering twice, with the final cake layer cut side down. Frost the cake with the buttercream, sprinkle the toasted coconut over the top and sides of the cake, and refrigerate for about 1 hour before serving.

Makes 16 servings

Tuile Cookies

Tuile cookies, thin crisp cookies that can be formed into a wide range of shapes, make an elegant and versatile garnish for desserts. Because the cookies are so thin, it's important that the batter be spread very evenly before baking, to avoid uneven cooking. One trick is to cut a template out of a thin piece of cardboard or the thin plastic lid from a large yogurt-type container. Spoon a little of the batter inside the cut-out and use a flat spatula to spread it out evenly up to the edges of the template, then lift off the template and repeat a few more times on the baking sheet. If spreading by hand, draw the spatula evenly over each cookie to smooth the surface before baking.

Chestnut Chocolate Mousse
with Orange Gelée

PAN PACIFIC HOTEL, VANCOUVER, BRITISH COLUMBIA

E xecutive pastry chef Ted Hara is an artist with his dessert creations. A light chocolate mousse embellished with chestnuts hides a flavor- and texture-contrasting orange gelée center. At the Pan Pacific, chef Hara finishes the outside of the dome with a spray of melted chocolate, replicated at home with a simple drizzle of chocolate.

Dome molds are certainly not a standard home kitchen item. Ramekins are a reasonable substitute. Or, if you have coffee cups that are half-dome shaped, they can be used as well; the dessert even can be served directly from the cups rather than unmolded.

Candied chestnuts, the beloved marrons glacés of France, are not consistently available, but you may find them in gourmet food shops, especially in winter. Otherwise, buy whole canned or jarred chestnuts, already cooked and peeled, and simmer them in a syrup of equal parts sugar and water for 20 to 30 minutes, then let them cool in the syrup before draining and chopping.

Orange Gelée

3 tablespoons cold water

2 teaspoons (1 envelope) unflavored gelatin powder

⅔ cup freshly squeezed orange juice

1 tablespoon sugar

2 tablespoons apricot preserves

1 teaspoon Cointreau or Grand Marnier

¼ teaspoon finely grated orange zest

Tuile Wave

¼ cup powdered sugar

3 tablespoons all-purpose flour

1 egg white

2 tablespoons unsalted butter, melted

¼ teaspoon finely grated orange zest

Crunchy Chocolate Disk

4 ounces top-quality milk chocolate, chopped

3 tablespoons finely ground toasted skinned hazelnuts

½ cup fine chocolate wafer cookie crumbs

Chestnut Chocolate Mousse

4½ ounces Valrhona Manjari or other top-quality bittersweet chocolate, chopped

2 egg yolks

4 ounces candied chestnuts, finely chopped (about ⅔ cup)

2 teaspoons Cointreau or Grand Marnier

1 cup whipping cream

2 ounces top-quality milk chocolate, chopped

For the orange gelée, put the cold water in a small saucepan, sprinkle the gelatin powder over, and set aside to soften, about 5 minutes. When soft, warm the gelatin over medium-low heat just until melted. Meanwhile, heat the orange juice and sugar in a small saucepan over medium-low heat until warmed and the sugar is dissolved, about 5 minutes. Stir the melted

gelatin into the orange juice, then stir in the apricot preserves (avoiding large pieces of fruit from the preserves), Cointreau, and orange zest. Pour the mixture into a 9- by 13-inch baking dish and refrigerate until set and firm, about 1 hour.

For the tuiles (see sidebar, page 178), sift together the sugar and flour into a medium bowl. Add the egg white and whisk well to blend. Add the melted butter and orange zest and whisk until smooth. Set the batter aside to rest for at least 1½ hours.

When the batter has rested, preheat the oven to 350°F. Line a baking sheet with a silicone baking mat or parchment paper.

Use a small offset spatula to spread a thin layer of batter in rectangles about 6 inches long and ¾ inch wide. Bake until the cookies are golden on the edges and the center is just beginning to color, 7 to 10 minutes. Set up 3 wooden spoons or other round-handled utensils about 1½ inches apart. Lift the cookies from the baking sheet and drape them over the handles to make a wave form. Let cool completely. Lift the cookies and set aside until ready to serve. You need 8 wave cookies in all.

For the chocolate disk, line a baking sheet with parchment paper. Melt the milk chocolate with the ground hazelnuts in the top of a double boiler or in a heatproof bowl set over a pan of simmering (not boiling) water, stirring until smooth. Add the cookie crumbs and stir to evenly mix. Spread the mixture about ⅛ inch thick on the prepared baking sheet and refrigerate until set, about 15 minutes. Cut into 8 circles the same size as the top of the molds you'll be using for the mousse. Keep refrigerated until ready to use.

Use a small sharp knife to cut the orange gelée into small dice, about ⅛-inch squares. With a rubber spatula, scoop the diced gelée into a small bowl and refrigerate until needed.

For the chocolate mousse, melt the bittersweet chocolate in the top of a double boiler or in a heatproof bowl set over a pan of simmering (not boiling) water, stirring until smooth. Take the chocolate from the heat, add the egg yolks, and whisk until smooth. Stir in the chopped chestnuts and the Cointreau. Whip the cream in an electric mixer at medium-high speed to soft peaks, then gently fold the whipped cream into the chocolate mixture.

To assemble, line eight 1-cup ramekins or other molds with plastic wrap, as neatly as possible (if using nonstick dome molds or serving the mousse directly from the dish, skip this step). Spoon about two-thirds of the chocolate-chestnut mousse into the molds, forming an indentation in the center. Spoon about 1 tablespoon of the diced orange gelée into each dish and top with the remaining mousse to just fill the mold. Refrigerate until set, at least 4 hours.

Shortly before serving, melt the milk chocolate in the top of a double boiler or in a small heatproof bowl set over a pan of simmering (not boiling) water, stirring until smooth. Transfer the melted chocolate to a pastry bag with a very small plain tip (or into a small resealable plastic bag from which you snip a very small hole in 1 lower corner of the bag). Press the cookie rounds on top of each mousse and unmold onto individual plates, using the plastic wrap to gently pull the mousse from the molds. Scatter some of the remaining orange gelée around the mousse and drizzle the tops of the mousses with the melted chocolate. Set the tuile waves on top of the mousse or lean them alongside, and serve right away.

Makes 8 servings

Figment of Your Imagination

Pastry chef Sue McCown is one of the most creative dessert divas around. This recipe is a perfect example of her work, bringing together top-quality ingredients—including fall's fresh Black Mission figs, locally made cheeses, candied pecans, and balsamic vinegar—in a whimsical dish that is as compelling to the eye as to the palate. You'll be amazed how much a flattened ripe fig resembles beef carpaccio. All the components can be made up to a day in advance and the dessert easily assembled just before serving.

Other hard cheese, such as Parmigiano-Reggiano, can be used in place of Washington's Samish Bay Montasio. Quark is a soft, unripened cow's milk cheese that is vaguely reminiscent of thick yogurt. McCown uses Quark from Appel Farms in Ferndale, Washington, available in many Northwest stores.

I pint fresh figs (about 16 figs), stems removed

I to 2 ounces Samish Bay Montasio cheese

Lemon and Quark Sorbet

¾ cup Quark

½ cup freshly squeezed lemon juice

½ cup lemon curd

½ cup light corn syrup

½ cup water

¼ cup sugar

¼ teaspoon salt

Balsamic Syrup

½ cup aged balsamic vinegar from Modena, such as 12-year-old Antica Italia

½ cup sugar

Candied Pecans

½ cup sugar

½ cup pecan halves

For the sorbet, combine ¼ cup of the Quark with the lemon juice, lemon curd, corn syrup, water, sugar, and salt in a large bowl and whisk until smooth. Freeze in an ice cream machine according to the manufacturer's instructions. Fold in the remaining ½ cup Quark, transfer the sorbet to an airtight container, and freeze until set, at least 2 hours.

For the balsamic syrup, combine the vinegar and sugar in a small saucepan and bring to a boil over medium-high heat, swirling the pan gently now and then to help the sugar dissolve. Reduce the heat to medium-low and simmer until the mixture looks thick and syrupy, 15 to 20 minutes. Set aside to cool.

For the candied pecans, put the sugar in a heavy saucepan over medium heat and stir with a wooden spoon until the sugar starts to melt. Increase the heat to medium-high and stop stirring. When the sugar starts to turn golden brown, add the nuts. Immediately remove the pan from the heat and stir to evenly coat the nuts in the caramel. Pour the candied nuts out onto a silicone baking mat or lightly oiled baking sheet and separate the nuts with a fork so they'll cool individually.

For the fig carpaccio, put 1 fig on top of a square piece of plastic wrap and lay another piece of plastic wrap over it. Use the flat bottom of a skillet to gently flatten the fig until it is paper thin, working in light strokes (pounding too hard may create holes). Set the flattened fig, still covered with plastic wrap, on a baking sheet. Repeat with the remaining figs, then put the baking sheet in the freezer until the figs are frozen, about 1 hour. Take 1 fig from the freezer and peel off 1 of the sheets of plastic. Gently press the fig onto a large dinner plate and peel off the plastic from the other side. Repeat with the remaining figs, slightly overlapping to cover the surface of the plate (about 4 figs per plate, depending on their size). Put the fig-covered plate back in the freezer until ready to serve. Repeat with 3 more plates.

Shortly before serving, take the plates from the freezer and let sit for about 10 minutes. Use a vegetable peeler to cut the cheese into long, thin curls. Set a generous scoop of lemon and Quark sorbet in the center of each plate, drizzle the balsamic syrup over the figs, and scatter with some of the candied pecans. Garnish with the cheese curls and serve right away.

MAKES 4 SERVINGS

Chocolate Fondant

Bernard Callebaut is the chocolate of choice for this simple but stunning dessert at The Aerie, though you can use other top-quality chocolate. Serve with creamy-rich vanilla ice cream to complement the intense chocolateness, or consider the Raspberry Swirl Ice Cream (page 168) or Star Anise Ice Cream (page 153). Extra chocolate ice cubes will make an ideal quick and rich hot chocolate: Combine ten or twelve of the cubes in a small saucepan with a mug's worth of milk and warm over medium heat, whisking occasionally.

8 ounces top-quality bittersweet chocolate, chopped

½ cup unsalted butter

5 eggs, separated

½ cup granulated sugar

⅓ cup finely ground almonds

⅓ cup all-purpose flour

⅓ cup cornstarch

¼ cup powdered sugar

Vanilla ice cream, for serving

Chocolate Ice Cubes

4 ounces top-quality bittersweet chocolate, chopped

⅔ cup whipping cream

3 tablespoons water

3 tablespoons unsalted butter, cut into small pieces

For the chocolate ice cubes, put the chocolate in a heatproof bowl. Combine the cream, water, and butter in a medium saucepan and bring just to a boil, stirring to help the butter melt. Pour the hot cream mixture over the chocolate and whisk to melt the chocolate. Let cool, whisking often. Pour the chocolate mixture into a loaf pan and freeze until solid, careful that the pan is sitting evenly so the chocolate will freeze in an even layer. Cut the frozen mixture into ½-inch cubes and return them to the freezer in a resealable plastic bag.

Preheat the oven to 350°F. Lightly oil a standard 12-cup muffin pan.

Combine the chocolate and butter in a medium saucepan over low heat and warm until melted, stirring occasionally, about 5 minutes. Take the pan from the heat and whisk in the egg yolks until smooth, then whisk in the granulated sugar, ground almonds, flour, cornstarch, and powdered sugar until evenly blended.

Whip the egg whites in an electric mixer at medium-high speed until soft peaks form. Gently fold one-quarter of the egg whites into the chocolate mixture to lighten it, then fold the chocolate into the remaining egg whites until evenly blended.

Half-fill each muffin cup with the chocolate batter, put a frozen chocolate ice cube in the center, and then top with more of the batter to fill the mold.

Bake until puffed and beginning to rise above the edge of the pans, about 15 minutes. Let the fondants cool for 10 minutes in the molds. Turn out the fondants and set them on individual plates. Serve warm, with a scoop of vanilla ice cream alongside.

MAKES 12 SERVINGS

Grand Marnier Cake

While a total indulgence, this airy sponge cake layered with fresh orange curd and cream cheese frosting still manages to be light. It's best to keep the cake well chilled after assembly, taking it from the refrigerator just before serving. The icing makes enough so that some can be spooned into a pastry bag fitted with a star tip and used to make a decorative edge around the top and bottom perimeter of the cake. When fresh local berries are in season, you could quickly toss some in Grand Marnier to serve alongside the cake.

8 eggs, separated

1 cup granulated sugar

¼ teaspoon vanilla extract

¼ teaspoon salt

2 cups sifted cake flour

Orange Curd

¾ cup granulated sugar

½ cup freshly squeezed orange juice

¼ cup freshly squeezed lemon and/or lime juice

3 whole eggs

3 egg yolks

1 tablespoon grated orange zest

1 teaspoon grated lemon and/or lime zest

¼ cup unsalted butter, cut into small pieces and chilled

¼ teaspoon vanilla extract

Pinch salt

Grand Marnier Syrup

¼ cup granulated sugar

¼ cup water

¼ cup freshly squeezed orange juice

¼ cup Grand Marnier

Splash of limoncello (optional)

Cream Cheese Icing

1 pound cream cheese, at room temperature

1 cup unsalted butter, at room temperature

6 cups powdered sugar, sifted; more if needed

Grated zest of two small oranges

3 tablespoons freshly squeezed orange juice

1½ teaspoons vanilla extract

Preheat the oven to 350°F. Line two 9-inch cake pans with rounds of parchment paper and set aside.

For the cake, beat the egg yolks in an electric mixer with ½ cup of the sugar until very thick and pale. Add the vanilla and mix to blend. In another bowl, beat the egg whites and salt to soft peaks and add the remaining ½ cup sugar. Beat until stiff and glossy. Fold half of the egg whites into the yolks, then fold in half of the flour. Fold in the remaining egg whites and the remaining flour. Pour the batter into the prepared pans and bake until light golden and the top springs back when lightly touched, about 20 minutes. Let the cakes cool on a wire rack.

For the curd, whisk together the sugar, juices, whole eggs, egg yolks, and zests in the top of a double boiler or in a heatproof bowl set over a pan of simmering (not boiling) water and cook until thick, whisking constantly, about 15 minutes. (The curd will turn opaque, the color changing from vivid yellow-orange to a softer tone.) When the curd is thick enough that a spoonful of it drizzled back into the bowl holds its shape for a few seconds, take the pan from the heat and whisk in the butter, vanilla, and salt. Pour the curd into a shallow dish, cover the surface of the curd with plastic wrap to prevent a skin from forming, and let cool. Refrigerate until fully chilled.

For the syrup, bring the sugar and water to a boil, stirring occasionally to dissolve the sugar. Stir in the juice, Grand Marnier, and limoncello (if using). Set aside to cool.

For the icing, cream together the cream cheese and butter in an electric mixer at medium speed. Add the powdered sugar, orange zest, orange juice, and vanilla and beat until smooth and creamy. Fold in 1 cup of the cooled orange curd. If the icing is quite soft, add another ½ cup to 1 cup of powdered sugar.

To assemble, use a serrated knife to cut both cake layers in half horizontally and put one half, cut side up, on a serving plate. Brush with ¼ cup of the syrup. Spread ½ cup of the icing on the cake and top with one-third of the curd. Repeat twice more. Set the final layer of cake on top, smooth side up, crumb side down. Brush some more syrup on the top layer and let it soak in. Frost the cake with the remaining icing and decorate with a pastry bag and tip if desired. Refrigerate for at least 3 hours before serving.

Makes 12 servings

Black and White Soufflé

THE GEORGIAN, SEATTLE, WASHINGTON

*N*othing makes quite the finale to a dinner party that a soufflé does, fresh from the oven and lighter than air. This recipe from executive chef Gavin Stephenson offers some hidden surprises—little pockets of melted chocolate within the soufflé. It's important to evenly butter the soufflé dishes; unbuttered spots will make the soufflé batter stick and not rise fully or evenly.

2 cups whole milk

1¼ cups sugar

¼ cup unsalted butter

½ cup all-purpose flour

5 eggs, separated

4 ounces top-quality white chocolate, chopped

4 ounces top-quality semisweet chocolate, chopped

Preheat the oven to 375°F. Butter six 1-cup individual soufflé dishes or ramekins, coat the insides with sugar, and tap to remove excess.

Combine the milk and ¼ cup of the sugar in a medium saucepan and bring just to a boil over medium-high heat. Melt the butter in a small saucepan over medium heat, whisk in the flour to make a smooth paste, and cook just until the mixture becomes lightly frothy, about 2 minutes. Whisk the paste into the milk mixture and cook over medium-high heat until thickened, 1 to 2 minutes, whisking often. Transfer this soufflé base to a mixer fitted with the paddle attachment and blend on low speed until cooled, about 15 minutes. Add the egg yolks and continue blending at low speed until evenly

mixed. Transfer to a large bowl and set aside. Thoroughly wash and dry the mixer bowl.

Whip the egg whites with an electric mixer at medium-high speed until frothy. Begin to gradually add the remaining 1 cup sugar, whipping constantly, until the egg whites are stiff and glossy. Fold one-third of the egg whites into the soufflé base to lighten it, then fold in the remaining egg whites. Finally, fold the white and semisweet chocolate pieces into the soufflé base and spoon it into the prepared soufflé dishes, to about ¼ inch below the rim.

Holding the rim of one of the dishes between your thumb and forefinger, draw your fingers around the outer edge to form a tidy rim to help with even rising. Set the dishes in a baking dish, set it on the oven rack, and half-fill the baking dish with boiling water. Bake until the soufflés are well risen and lightly browned on top, 25 to 30 minutes. Carefully transfer the soufflés to small plates and serve right away.

MAKES 6 SERVINGS

Trifle

There are countless variations on this classic English dessert. This recipe is quite traditional, with a good drizzle of cream sherry imbibing the cake, layered with rich custard and fresh berries. By tradition, trifle is made in a clear glass dish to show off the jelly-roll slices and layering of ingredients. Prepared jelly rolls, available in the bakery section of most grocery stores, make a great shortcut for this recipe. Or, certainly feel free to make your own jelly roll by spreading a thin sponge cake with raspberry jam before rolling it into a tight cylinder.

About 12 ounces jelly roll (sponge cake with strawberry or raspberry filling)

1 cup cream sherry

½ cup toasted sliced almonds

2 cups fresh berries (such as blueberries, sliced strawberries, raspberries)

1 cup whipping cream

Custard

¾ cup sugar

1 tablespoon all-purpose flour

¼ teaspoon salt

5 eggs, lightly beaten

3 cups milk, warmed

2 teaspoons vanilla extract

For the custard, combine the sugar, flour, and salt in a heavy saucepan. Add the eggs and mix well with a wooden spoon. Stir in the warm milk and cook over medium heat, stirring, until thick enough to coat the back of the spoon,

6 to 8 minutes. Take the pan from the heat and stir in the vanilla. Strain the custard through a fine sieve and refrigerate until thoroughly chilled.

Cut the jelly roll into slices about ¾ inch thick and cover the bottom of a 2-quart serving dish with half of the slices. Sprinkle ½ cup of the sherry over the cake. Pour half of the cooled custard over the cake, sprinkle with half the almonds, and top with half of the berries. Cover with another layer of cake, sprinkle with the remaining sherry, and top with the remaining custard. Whip the cream to soft peaks and spread it over the custard. Sprinkle the remaining almonds over and arrange the remaining berries on top. Cover with plastic wrap and refrigerate until ready to serve, scooping the trifle out into individual bowls.

Makes 8 to 12 servings

Strawberry and White Chocolate Sponge Cake with Dark Chocolate Glaze

Aqua Riva, Vancouver, British Columbia

ote that you must make the white chocolate cream several hours before you assemble the cake, preferably the day before, so plan ahead. For ease in handling the cake while assembling and decorating, cut a round of sturdy cardboard the same size as the base of the springform pan and cover the cardboard neatly with foil. You can also simply assemble the cake on the serving plate, though the chocolate glaze will pool around the base of the cake and the finished look won't be as tidy. This cake is best enjoyed the day that you make it.

6 whole eggs

1 egg yolk

½ cup sugar

½ teaspoon vanilla extract

½ cup all-purpose flour

2 cups thinly sliced fresh strawberries, plus more for garnish

½ cup top-quality white chocolate, chopped

White Chocolate Cream

1 pound top-quality white chocolate, coarsely chopped

1½ cups whipping cream

Dark Chocolate Glaze

8 ounces top-quality semisweet chocolate, coarsely chopped

1 cup whipping cream

5 tablespoons unsalted butter

4 teaspoons sugar

For the white chocolate cream, put the white chocolate in a heatproof bowl. Bring the whipping cream to just below a boil in a small saucepan over medium-high heat and pour it over the chocolate. Whisk the mixture until the chocolate is melted and completely smooth. Refrigerate until fully chilled, 3 to 4 hours or, preferably, overnight.

Preheat the oven to 350°F. Line the bottom of a 10-inch springform pan with a round of parchment paper.

Put 3 of the whole eggs and the egg yolk in the bowl of an electric mixer. Separate the remaining 3 eggs, putting the yolks in with the other eggs and setting aside the 3 whites in a separate bowl. Add the sugar and vanilla to the eggs and beat on medium-high speed until the mixture thickens, 8 to 10 minutes. Sift the flour over the eggs and use a spatula to gently fold it into the batter. Whip the egg whites with an electric mixer at high speed (or with a large whisk) until they form soft peaks. Gently fold the egg whites into the batter and pour the batter into the prepared pan. Bake until lightly browned on top and the cake springs back when gently pressed with your finger, 25 to 30 minutes. Let the cake cool in the pan on a wire rack for 10 minutes. Take the cake from the pan, discard the parchment paper, and lightly wrap the cake in plastic. Refrigerate until ready to use. (The cake can be made up to 2 days in advance.)

For the dark chocolate glaze, put the chocolate in a heatproof bowl. Combine the cream, butter, and sugar in a small saucepan and bring to a boil over medium-high heat, stirring occasionally to help the sugar dissolve. Pour the hot cream mixture over the chocolate and whisk until the chocolate is melted

and completely smooth. Set aside to cool slightly at room temperature while you assemble the cake.

Take the cake from the refrigerator and use a serrated knife to cut it into 2 layers. Put one of the layers cut side up on a cardboard round or on the serving plate.

Whip the white chocolate cream in an electric mixer at medium-high speed until light but firm. Spread half of the white chocolate cream on the cake layer and cover with an even layer of the sliced strawberries. Spread the rest of the white chocolate cream over the berries, top with the second cake layer, cut side down, and press gently. Use a metal spatula to smooth the sides of the cake, so that the cream and berries form an even edge with the cake.

If the cake is on a cardboard round, carefully set it on a wire rack on top of a rimmed baking sheet. Slowly pour the glaze evenly over the cake and use a metal spatula to spread it over the top and sides of the cake. (If finishing the cake on its serving plate, you may want to use less of the glaze.) Put the cake in the refrigerator to let the glaze set, about 15 minutes.

Meanwhile, put the chopped white chocolate in a small bowl and set it over a pan of simmering (not boiling) water, stirring until it is melted and smooth. Pour the melted chocolate into a piping bag with a small plain tip (or into a small resealable plastic bag from which you snip a very small hole in a lower corner of the bag). Take the cake from the refrigerator and drizzle with the melted white chocolate, in any pattern you like. Refrigerate the cake for at least another 10 minutes, or up to 2 hours, before serving.

Cut the cake into wedges, garnished with strawberry slices on top if you like.

Makes 12 servings

Chocolate and Pistachio Domes

D ome molds are a specialty item of upscale pastry kitchens, but are not found in most home kitchens. If you are a devoted pastry maker, you can hunt down some silicone dome molds through specialty food stores—or simply use ramekins.

Pistachio paste is another specialty item used in baking, a very concentrated paste of ground nuts. It is available from baking supply outlets such as King Arthur Flour. You can instead start with roasted pistachios and grind them yourself at home, though the flavor won't be quite as pronounced.

Chocolate Cake

2½ ounces top-quality bittersweet chocolate, chopped

5 tablespoons unsalted butter, at room temperature

2 eggs, separated

2½ tablespoons sugar

Pistachio Bavarian Mousse

1 egg yolk

¼ cup sugar

¼ cup milk

1 tablespoon pistachio paste or 2 tablespoons very finely ground toasted pistachios

1 teaspoon unflavored gelatin powder

2 tablespoons cold water

1 cup whipping cream, whipped to soft peaks

Chocolate Mousse

8 ounces top-quality bittersweet chocolate, chopped

¼ cup milk

2 egg yolks

⅓ cup sugar

2 tablespoons water

1¼ cups whipping cream, whipped to soft peaks

Preheat the oven to 375°F. Line a 9- by 13-inch baking pan with parchment paper for the chocolate cake. Line an 8-inch round pan with plastic wrap for the pistachio mousse.

For the chocolate cake, melt the chocolate and butter in the top of a double boiler or in a heatproof bowl set over a pan of simmering (not boiling) water, stirring until smooth. Take the pan from the heat. In a separate bowl, whisk together the egg yolks and 1 tablespoon of the sugar until pale yellow and thick. Whip the egg whites with the remaining 1½ tablespoons sugar to stiff peaks. Fold the yolks into the chocolate mixture, then gently fold in the whites. Pour the batter into the prepared baking pan and bake until it springs back when lightly touched in the center, 8 to 10 minutes. Set aside to cool on a wire rack. Cut out eight 3-inch circles of cake.

For the pistachio Bavarian mousse, whisk together the egg yolk and 1 table-spoon of the sugar in a medium bowl until pale and light. Bring the milk, the remaining 3 tablespoons sugar, and pistachio paste to a boil in a small saucepan over medium-high heat, whisking often. Add a few tablespoons of the hot milk to the egg yolk and whisk well, then add the remaining milk and whisk together. Pour the mixture back into the saucepan and cook over low heat, stirring constantly, until thickened, about 5 minutes. Take the pan

from the heat. Sprinkle the gelatin over the cold water in a small dish and set aside to soften, about 5 minutes. Add the softened gelatin to the saucepan and whisk until melted and smooth. Set aside to cool to lukewarm. Fold in the whipped cream. Pour the mixture into the prepared pan and freeze until firm. Cut into eight 2-inch rounds.

For the chocolate mousse, melt the chocolate with the milk in the top of a double boiler or in a heatproof bowl set over a pan of simmering (not boiling) water, stirring until smooth; take the pan from the heat. Whip the egg yolks in an electric mixer at medium-high speed until well blended. In a very small saucepan over medium heat, cook the sugar and water until the sugar is melted, stirring occasionally. Increase the heat to medium-high and cook, without stirring, to 240°F (use a candy thermometer to be sure). With the mixer at medium-low speed, slowly pour the syrup into the yolks and blend until cool. Add the yolk mixture to the chocolate and mix until smooth. Gently fold in the whipped cream and put the mousse into a pastry bag fitted with a large plain tip.

If using ramekins, line eight ½-cup ramekins with plastic wrap, as neatly as possible. Half-fill eight 3-inch dome molds or the ramekins with chocolate mousse. Put a round of pistachio mousse in the center, and top with the remaining chocolate mousse. Cover with a circle of chocolate cake and gently press down. Freeze the molds overnight. Unmold the desserts onto individual serving plates. Refrigerate for about an hour to soften slightly before serving.

MAKES 8 SERVINGS

Appendix: Restaurants & Inns

A TOUCH OF EUROPE™
BED AND BREAKFAST
220 North 16th Avenue
Yakima, WA 98902
509-454-9775 / 888-438-7073
www.winesnw.com/toucheuropeb&b.htm

THE AERIE
600 Ebedora Lane
Malahat, BC V0R 2L0
250-443-7115 / 800-518-1933
www.aerie.bc.ca

AQUA RIVA
200 Granville Street
Vancouver, BC V6C 1S4
604-683-5599
www.aquariva.com

THE ARBOR CAFE
380 High Street NE
Salem, OR 97301
503-588-2353

BACCHUS RISTORANTE
Wedgewood Hotel
845 Hornby Street
Vancouver, BC V6Z 1V1
604-689-7777 / 800-663-0666
www.wedgewoodhotel.com

BALDWIN SALOON
205 Court Street
The Dalles, OR 97058
541-296-5666

BARKING FROG
Willows Lodge
14580 NE 145th Street
Woodinville, WA 98072
425-424-3900 / 877-424-3930
www.willowslodge.com

BEDDIS HOUSE BED AND BREAKFAST
131 Miles Avenue
Salt Spring Island, BC V8K 2E1
250-537-1028 / 866-537-1028
www.beddishousebandb.com

BUGATTI'S RISTORANTE
18740 Willamette Drive
West Linn, OR 97068
503-636-9555

CAFE BRIO
944 Fort Street
Victoria, BC V8V 3K2
250-383-0009 / 866-270-5461
www.cafe-brio.com

CANLIS
2576 Aurora Avenue N
Seattle, WA 98109
206-283-3313
www.canlis.com

THE CANNERY SEAFOOD HOUSE
2205 Commissioner Street
Vancouver, BC V5L 1A4
604-254-9606 / 877-254-9606
www.canneryseafood.com

CANYON WAY RESTAURANT AND BOOKSTORE
1216 SW Canyon Way
Newport, OR 97365
541-265-8319

CAPRIAL'S BISTRO
7015 SE Milwaukie Avenue
Portland, OR 97202
503-236-6457
www.caprial.com

CASCADIA
2328 First Avenue
Seattle, WA 98121
206-448-8884
www.cascadiarestaurant.com

CHANTICLEER INN
120 Gresham Street
Ashland, OR 97520
541-482-1919 / 800-898-1950
www.ashland-bed-breakfast.com

DAHLIA LOUNGE
2001 Fourth Avenue
Seattle, WA 98121
206-682-4142
www.tomdouglas.com/dahlia

DIVA AT THE MET
The Metropolitan Hotel
645 Howe Street
Vancouver, BC V6C 2Y9
604-602-7788
www.metropolitan.com/diva

DUCK SOUP INN
50 Duck Soup Lane
Friday Harbor, WA 98250
360-378-4878
www.ducksoupinn.com

DURLACHER HOF
7055 Nesters Road
Whistler, BC V0N 1B7
604-932-1924 / 877-932-1924
www.durlacherhof.com

EARTH AND OCEAN
W Hotel
1112 Fourth Avenue
Seattle, WA 98101
206-264-6060
www.earth-oceanrestaurant.com

FIRST STREET HAVEN
107 E First Street
Port Angeles, WA 98362
360-457-0352

FOLEY STATION
1114 Adams Avenue
La Grande, OR 97850
541-963-7473
www.foleystation.com

FROM THE BAYOU
508 Garfield Street
Parkland, WA 98444
253-539-4269
www.fromthebayou.com

GEISER GRAND HOTEL
1996 Main Street
Baker City, OR 97814
541-523-1889 / 888-434-7374
www.geisergrand.com

THE GEORGIAN
The Fairmont Olympic Hotel
411 University Street
Seattle, WA 98101
206-621-1700
www.fairmont.com/seattle

HARRISON HOUSE BED AND BREAKFAST
2310 NW Harrison Boulevard
Corvallis, OR 97330
541-752-6248 / 800-233-6248
www.corvallis-lodging.com

HIGGINS RESTAURANT AND BAR
1239 SW Broadway
Portland, OR 97205
503-222-9070

HIGHLAND INN
439 Hannah Road
Friday Harbor, WA 98250
360-378-9450 / 888-400-9850
www.highlandinn.com

HUDSON'S BAR AND GRILL
The Heathman Lodge
7801 NE Greenwood Drive
Vancouver, WA 98662
360-816-6100
www.heathmanlodge.com

HUNT CLUB
Sorrento Hotel
900 Madison Street
Seattle, WA 98104
206-343-6156
www.huntclub-seattle.com

JACKSONVILLE INN
175 E California Street
Jacksonville, OR 97530
541-899-1900 / 800-321-9344
www.jacksonvilleinn.com

KASTEEL FRANSSEN
33575 Highway 20
Oak Harbor, WA 98277
360-675-0724

LINDAMAN'S GOURMET BISTRO
1235 S Grand Boulevard
Spokane, WA 99204
509-839-3000
www.lindamans.com

MANNING PARK RESORT
7500 Highway 3
Manning Provincial Park
Hope, BC V0X 1L0
250-840-8822 / 800-330-3321
www.manningparkresort.com

MARZANO
516 Garfield S
Parkland, WA 98444
253-537-4191

MONSOON
615 19th Avenue E
Seattle, WA 98112
206-325-2111

MOUNTAIN HOME LODGE
8201 Mountain Home Road
Leavenworth, WA 98826
509-548-7077 / 800-414-2378
www.mthome.com

PACIFIC CAFE
100 N Commercial Street
Bellingham, WA 98225
360-647-0800

PALACE KITCHEN
2030 Fifth Avenue
Seattle, WA 98121
206-448-2001
www.tomdouglas.com/palace

PAN PACIFIC VANCOUVER
300-999 Canada Place
Vancouver, BC V6C 3B5
604-662-8111
www.vancouver.panpacific.com

THE PLACE BAR AND GRILL
1 Spring Street
Friday Harbor, WA 98250
360-378-8707

QUATTRO ON FOURTH
2611 West 4th Avenue
Vancouver, B.C. V6K 1P8
604-734-4444
www.quattrorestaurants.com

SARATOGA INN
201 Cascade Avenue
Langley, WA 98260
360-221-5801 / 800-698-2910
www.foursisters.com/inns/
saratogainn.html

THE SHOALWATER RESTAURANT
Shelburne Inn
4415 Pacific Way
Seaview, WA 98644
360-642-4142 / 800-INN-1896
www.shoalwater.com

SOUTH BAY BED AND BREAKFAST
4095 South Bay Drive
Lake Whatcom
Sedro-Woolley, WA 98284
360-595-2086 / 877-595-2086
www.southbaybb.com

STRATFORD MANOR BED & BREAKFAST
4566 Anderson Way
Bellingham, WA 98226
360-715-8441 / 800-240-6779
www.stratfordmanor.com

THE TEAHOUSE IN STANLEY PARK
7501 Stanley Park Drive
Vancouver, BC V6G 3E2
604-669-3281 / 800-280-9893
www.sequoiarestaurants.com/teahouse_
about.html

THIRD FLOOR FISH CAFE
205 Lake Street S
Kirkland, WA 98033
425-822-3553
www.fishcafe.com

TOJO'S
777 W Broadway
Vancouver, BC V5Z 4J7
604-872-8050
www.tojos.com

TURTLEBACK FARM INN
1981 Crow Valley Road
Eastsound, WA 98245
360-376-4914 / 800-376-4914
www.turtlebackinn.com

WEST
2881 Granville Street
Vancouver, BC V6H 3J4
604-738-8938
www.westrestaurant.com

THE WHITEHOUSE-CRAWFORD RESTAURANT
55 W Cherry Street
Walla Walla, WA 99362
509-525-2222
www.whitehousecrawford.com

WILDWOOD RESTAURANT
1221 NW 21st Avenue
Portland, OR 97209
503-248-9663
www.wildwoodrestaurant.com

YARROW BAY GRILL
1270 Carillon Point
Kirkland, WA 98033
425-889-9052
www.ybbeachcafe.com

Index

A

Aerie, The, 202
    Chocolate Fondant, 186–87
    Roasted Pears with Szechwan
        Pepper and Bittersweet
        Chocolate Sauce, 80–83
almond
    Almond Cookie Crust, 120–22
    Almond Pear Clafouti, 63
    Almond Tea Cake, 27–28
    Chocolate Nut Pie, 135–36
    Sarah Bernhardts, 103–4
anise
    Star Anise Ice Cream, 153
apple
    Apple-Cranberry Pudding with
        Caramel Sauce, 78–79
    Braeburn Apples with a Walnut
        Filling Baked in Pommeau,
        72–73
    Deep Dish Apple Pie, 118–19
Apricot Cake, 74–75
Aqua Riva, 202
    Lemon Tart, 139–41
    Strawberry and White Chocolate
        Sponge Cake with Dark
        Chocolate Glaze, 195–98
Arbor Cafe, The, 202
    Oregon Berry Cheesecake,
        90–91

B

Bacchus Ristorante, 202
    Lemon Olive Oil Cake, 4–5
Baileys Glaze, 94–95
Baldwin Saloon, 202
    Chocolate-Covered Cherry
        Martini, 105
    Deep Dish Apple Pie, 118–19
balsamic vinegar
    Balsamic-Port Reduction, 61
    Balsamic Syrup, 184

banana
    Banana Cake, 29–30
    Hazelnut Chocolate Banana
        Cream Pie, 127–29
Barking Frog, 202
    Lemon Pudding Cake with
        Blackberry–Pinot Noir
        Coulis, 16–18
Basil Panna Cotta with Strawberries,
    48–49
Bayou Cheesecake, 34–35
Beddis House Bed and Breakfast,
    202
    Hazelnut Torte, 66–67
    Trifle, 193–94
berries
    Apple-Cranberry Pudding with
        Caramel Sauce, 78–79
    Basil Panna Cotta with
        Strawberries, 48–49
    Blackberry–Pinot Noir Coulis,
        17
    Blueberry Sauce, 106–7
    Chocolate Decadence with
        Strawberry Sauce, 32–33
    Chocolate Raspberry Cake,
        23–24
    Fresh Blueberry Tart with
        Lavender Crème Fraîche,
        120–23
    Frozen Strawberry and Lemon
        Terrine, 161–62
    Individual Rustic Blackberry
        Tarts, 130–31
    Marionberry Phyllo, 69–71
    Orange Cranberry Torte,
        19–20
    Oregon Berry Cheesecake,
        90–91
    Rainier Pavlova with Douglas
        Fir Sorbet and Macerated
        Berries, 150–52
    Raspberry Hazelnut Meringue,
        76–77

    Raspberry Swirl Ice Cream,
        168–69
    Red, White, and Blue
        Shortcakes, 106–8
    Summer Berry Shortcake,
        60–62
    in Trifle, 193–94
    Wild Huckleberry Crûme
        Brûlée, 38–39
    Wildflower Honey–Roasted
        Strawberries with Fennel
        Seed Blinis, 64–65
biscotti
    Pistachio-Orange Biscotti,
        100–2
Black and White Soufflé, 191–92
Black Bear Ginger Cake, 13–15
blackberry
    Blackberry–Pinot Noir Coulis,
        16–18
    Individual Rustic Blackberry
        Tarts, 130–31
    Marionberry Phyllo, 69–71
    Oregon Berry Cheesecake,
        90–91
    See also berries
blini
    Fennel Seed Blinis, 64–65
blueberry
    Blueberry Sauce, 106–7
    Fresh Blueberry Tart with
        Lavender Crème Fraîche,
        120–23
    Red, White, and Blue
        Shortcakes, 106–8
bombe
    White Chocolate and Pumpkin
        Bombe, 172–74
bread pudding
    Bread Pudding with Plum-Port
        Sauce, 56–57
    Chocolate and Brandied Dried
        Cherry Bread Pudding,
        42–44

Pudding, Double Chocolate Chip Cookies, and a luxurious Chocolate Hazelnut Torte. There is even a handful of after-dinner cocktails—a grown-ups-only option for capping off your time around the dinner table with spirit.

As ever with the Best Places cookbooks I have compiled, these recipes were all test-run in my home kitchen, so you can feel comfortable that they are presented with the home cook in mind. You can, however, count on some interesting insights from the chefs about the techniques and ingredients they use. The book serves as a tasty glimpse into some of the Northwest's best kitchens to see how chefs bring to life those desserts we love so much. Enjoy!

—*Cynthia C. Nims*

Introduction

The sweet tooth is a universal and undeniable force. Whether concluding dinner or accompanying that late-morning cup of coffee, a little bite of something sweet is just the thing we rely on for the kind of satisfaction only a sugary treat can bring. It makes sense that to find some of the best dessert recipes in the Northwest we'd return to those Best Places that we count on to feed us so well in this region.

All of the restaurants, cafes, and other eating establishments in the fourteenth edition of the *Best Places® Northwest* guidebook were invited to participate in this cookbook. What came of that invitation is a collection of 80 recipes that span the seasons, difficulty levels, and moods, from the pure comfort food of a Deep Dish Apple Pie to brownies charged up with espresso to the special-occasion extravagance of Coconut Cream Cake.

The seasonal scope of the Northwest's signature ingredients is well represented in these pages. Appearing among the first hints of springtime are the ruby stalks of rhubarb, and summer's kaleidoscope of berries provides endless inspiration for recipes from a simple nectarine cobbler to a silky crème brûlée embellished with wild huckleberries. Toasted hazelnuts, tart cranberries, juicy pears, and crisp apples evoke the cozy and warming cuisine of fall and winter. And when is it *not* the season for chocolate? Chocoholics will be well served with recipes the likes of Chocolate Gelato, Chocolate and Brandied Dried-Cherry Bread

Acknowledgments

Many thanks to the recipe testers who helped fine-tune this collection of dessert recipes: Jeff Ashley, Barbara Nims, and Anne Nisbet. It's not only their love of cooking, but also their critical eye for detail that I appreciate so much! Leora Bloom's assistance across the board—testing, editing, compiling, corresponding—was a godsend. Sincere thanks to you as well!